SACRED HEARTS RISING

FINDING YOUR WINGS

ESSAYS OF LOSS, TRAUMA, PAIN, AND SURVIVAL

COMPILED BY
BRENDA HAMMON

bhc
press™

Livonia, Michigan

Front cover artwork by Riëtte Delport, ©RuT. Used by permission. All rights reserved worldwide.

Scripture quotations taken from Holy Bible, New International Version®, NIV® Copyright ©1973, 1978, 1984, 2011 by Biblica, Inc.® Used by permission. All rights reserved worldwide.

Edited by Jen Violi and Amanda Lewis

SACRED HEARTS RISING: FINDING YOUR WINGS

Published by BHC Press

Library of Congress Control Number: 2018950988

ISBN: 978-1-948540-00-1 (Softcover)
ISBN: 978-1-948540-01-8 (Ebook)

Visit the publisher:
www.bhcpress.com

Also available in the
Sacred Hearts Rising series

Sacred Hearts Rising: Breaking the Silence One Story at a Time

Acknowledgments

I would like to take a moment to acknowledge a few people who have helped shape *Sacred Hearts Rising: Finding Your Wings*.

Riëtte Delport, once again, your amazing artwork is gracing the cover. Thank you for seeing my vison for a better world through our stories. I am honored.

Jen Violi, for all your dedication and focus on helping everyone tell their inspiring stories.

Colleen Songs, for creating forever poems from each story for the authors.

Bud, the man who has stood beside me through thick and thin, never wavering. You give me strength when I need it and then stand back while I soar. Love you for being you.

To everyone else who believed in the concept of these books and the Sacred Hearts Rising Community, who encouraged, supported, and embodied this remarkable journey, I thank you, for we can change the world one story at a time.

Note to the Reader

This book is not intended to dispense psychological or therapeutic advice. The information is provided for educational and inspirational purposes only. In the event you use any of the information in this book for yourself, which is your constitutional right, the author and publisher assume no responsibility for your actions. Although the author(s) and publisher have made every effort to ensure that the information in this book was correct at press time, the author(s) and publisher do not assume and hereby declaim any liability to any party for any loss, damage, or disruption by errors or omission, whether such error and omission result from negligence, accidents, or any other cause.

Table of Contents

Preface

It is with utmost pleasure that I bring to you this second Sacred Hearts Rising book, *Finding Your Wings*. Last year, after finishing *Sacred Hearts Rising: Breaking the Silence One Story at a Time*, I wasn't sure what would come next. I had a feeling I wanted to put forward a second anthology, but the first one seemed so full and covered so much territory that I wasn't sure where else we could go. I wondered if it was possible that more stories would come tumbling forward, begging to be told, begging to be released from within the confines of hearts and minds.

The stories came.

I was both saddened and amazed to see new and unique stories put forward by women and men for this anthology. Sad because these stories exist, sad at what one human being can do to another, that so many predators and perpetrators get away with what they have done. Sad that life presents challenges that can, at times, be insurmountable. Sad that so many humans are forced to suffer in silence.

On the other hand, I was amazed at the resilience, determination, strength, and passion I saw as each writer shared what has happened to them and how they've dealt with challenges, suffering, and the many versions of the crappy side of life. These are truly remarkable human beings. Both what the writers have endured and the gifts they share are astonishing.

I am honored that each writer placed their trust in me to help deliver their messages and experiences to the world, in the hopes that this sharing will help another person out there who may be alone and shouldering a similar burden.

Sacred Hearts Rising has become more than just another anthology; it has become a community of support for those who have shared their stories. A place where we all can feel free to talk about our lives and know that someone else gets us. This has become a place where our stories can be put to rest, where we can connect with others, and where we can thrive if we choose to.

Sacred Hearts Rising: Finding Your Wings builds on the foundation of the first book, as a new gathering place for stories, as well as a jumping off point. My hope for all of these writers is that in the sharing of their stories, they continue to find their own wings and take flight into something bigger and brighter—a new experience, or a new way to think and grow.

Within *Sacred Hearts Rising: Finding Your Wings*, you will read a wide variety of stories told by an equally wide variety of people. Like a special and elaborate meal, this is a compilation of incredible flavors, true voices, and true stories. As you follow the words lovingly dished out in these pages, you'll get a taste of who each of the storytellers are—their own style of writing, and the essence of their soul.

I invite you to take your time with this feast, and to savor the flavor of each person's unique story and journey to forgiving, accepting, and healing.

If, as you read these stories, you feel the desire to contribute your own, please visit us at *www.sacredheartsrising.com*, because you are so worth it, and there's always room at the table for one more.

Brenda Hammon

Foreword

When I was a girl growing up in Pittsburgh, Pennsylvania, books and stories were my beloved companions. One of my favorite summer activities was going to Northland Library every week or two with my mom and sisters, and checking out a stack of stories to devour. It wasn't unusual for me to come home with a dozen books—novels, collections of fairy tales, books on Greek mythology, whatever I could get my hands on.

Sometimes, my mom would declare quiet reading hour, and we'd all retreat to our various corners with our respective books. For a kid who would have been on board for quiet reading *days*, those hours were golden. I loved when we were all reading, separate but together. The energy, calm and focused. As if the stories held us all in a great big blanket fort, a much larger version of the girl-sized blanket fort that actually contained me while I read.

While I can call upon a multitude of other sweet and delightful memories, my childhood was also defined by having a chronically ill parent who died when I was fourteen. In the midst of all of the fear and anxiety I felt as my dad suffered with lupus for nine years, and in the midst of the heartbreak and grief as we lost him to cancer, one of the places I could always find sanctuary was inside a story.

I flailed, and stories held me. I hungered, and stories fed me. I despaired, and stories restored my hope. My heart broke, and stories healed me.

Since then, I've studied, practiced, and immersed myself in writing. I wrote a novel and had it published. Now I teach and facilitate writing workshops and retreats. I do developmental editing of books, and I mentor writers as they craft those books. In all of this, what I've learned is that story is not only individual but also collective medicine. Reading or writing alone still offers me deep healing, a particular kind of solace and relief. And when a group gathers to share stories, well, the cumulative invigorating effect is astounding.

When I facilitate workshops, I always offer at least one prompt, then all the writers in the room retreat to our various corners, much like my mom and sisters and I did for quiet reading hour. Except that instead of reading, we're writing. Diving into the prompt and letting the words spill out. While we write together, I can feel the stories holding us. The sounds of our pens merging into a pulsing hymn. After a while— twenty, thirty, forty minutes—we gather to share our work out loud. While we read and listen together, I can still feel the stories holding us. Holding our tears and laughter, our pasts and presents, our heartaches and joys.

My intention is always for us to co-create a sanctuary for stories and for the people who need to tell them, and each time we do, it covers my arms with goosebumps, fills my eyes with tears, and runs like an electric current through my blood.

There's nothing like it.

Or so I thought, until Brenda Hammon asked me to be the developmental editor for Sacred Hearts Rising, a new project she'd created to make space for women to share their stories. In the summer and fall of 2017, as I gave editorial feedback to twenty-five writers, as we sent drafts back and forth, listening to what each essay wanted to be, honing structures and sentences, I learned a new way of stories becoming collective medicine and creating a sacred container.

Now in the summer and fall of 2018, I've experienced the same thing for this second sacred and full-hearted anthology. Once again, Brenda worked hard to invite, gather, and organize offerings from a wide range of contributors, from seasoned writers to those crafting their very first pieces. All of these contributors, this time women and men, went off to their various corners, attending to their various stories, and wrote with a common intention: to offer words that lift hearts. It has been my honor and sacred task not only to support them in that intention through editing, but also to witness how everyone involved in this book has co-created something that held us all and now, we hope, will hold you, too.

So, welcome to this house that stories built. We're all so grateful you're here.

Know that as much as these stories are solid and sturdy, they are also dynamic and alive. As you hold this book, don't be surprised if it holds you back and fires you up.

In these pages, know that you won't find easy stories. The contributors to this book have known serious trauma and profound loss and pain. And they are more than their trauma. Much more. These essays were labored over with great love, born of bravery, fueled by transformation, and are bursting with beauty, hope, and passion. Together, they make a full and complex fire.

Like logs, sticks, and twigs in such a fire, these essays seem to warm each other, a spark from one flying to ignite another quickly, sweet scenes or funny snapshots flashing up and out in a whoosh, like kindling. Then bigger moments and journeys, the slow burners. Once those logs get going, they can keep a reader warm for a long time. A reader like you. Sometimes the smoke may make your eyes water, or the heat might get a bit intense. That's the way of fires, and it is okay to step away and come back when you're ready.

If you're flailing, may these stories hold you! If you're hungry, may these stories feed you! If you're despairing, may these stories restore your hope! And if your heart is broken, may these stories offer you healing, and breath, and wings.

Jen Violi
Author, Editor, Story Mentor

"We are ordinary people sharing extraordinary stories."
~ Brenda Hammon ~

All Things Work Together for the Good
by Shey Hennig

"...to all who mourn...he will bestow a crown of beauty for ashes..."
Isaiah 61:3

My daughter's favorite author, C.S. Lewis, said, "Isn't it funny how day by day nothing changes, but when you look back, everything is different?" I am fifty-two years old, wife to the best person I know, a mother of two, an accredited business woman, and a lover of Jesus. I wake up in the morning and feel a sense of gratitude for the day ahead. I publish my daily Facebook encouragement, pour some coffee, pick out an outfit I don't feel terrible in, listen to a podcast with my husband, and head out the door.

There are times when the day feels stale, with another scoop from the same coffee can—another email sent, another bill on the counter, another dinner party, another discussion about the mortgage. But C.S. Lewis was on to something, because when I take the moment necessary to look back, I see that everything has changed and continues to change constantly.

My kids are adults, moving out and getting married, my debts have been paid off, my joints hurt a bit more than last month, I speak with more confidence and surety, I stand straighter for the things that matter to me; people my age are needing their skin lifted or their blood pressure lowered, and everything is different. Still, I have grown to know that no matter what changes, or even stays the same, I have a deep acceptance and wholeness in my very being that all is, and always will be, well with my soul.

If I choose to look way back, I can imagine a fourteen-year-old girl in Ireland during the year 1966, preparing to bring her newborn baby to Canada to be adopted. As a mother, I can imagine the fierce instinct to protect that baby, the love for this person you've spent nine months growing and keeping with every beat of your heart. What I can't imagine is how incredibly painful it would be to place her in the arms of someone else, to have the records sealed, and to say a final goodbye.

That girl was my mother. I was placed in foster care in 1966, without name, without family, and seemingly, without hope. I don't know who that girl became, but I appreciate her decision and her courage, and yet struggle at moments to understand how a mother could do such a thing. I spent a brief time in the loving home of a couple whom I met again later in life and whom I hold in highest regard, and I was eventually adopted into the home of the man and woman I call mother and father to this day. They have loved me, cared for me, provided for me, and instilled in me a strength, a sturdiness, a voice.

There is a great bitter sweetness that breeds in the heart and innocence of an adopted child. How else can you feel at times, but utterly abandoned?

When I was growing up, being bullied, feeling too different, my mother, faithfully, would tell me that I was incredibly wanted, handpicked, chosen. Yet somehow, I still felt such a sense of being unwanted and unworthy and sought acceptance in places I never found it. I entered into many relationships, relationships so unhealthy and abusive. It was that looking-for-love-in-all-the-wrong-places syndrome, somehow believing that the sense of rejection I felt could be made up for in the arms of someone else.

I had sensed an emptiness my whole life. As a child, I seemed to have unfounded fears. Fears of the dark, the stillness, and certainly, the unknown. My mom would take me to church on holidays, occasions, and the frequent Sunday, and it seemed to bring a peace to me. There seemed to be a void in me that church would temporarily fill, but never completely.

When I was about twenty-five years old, I found myself struggling with another failed relationship, one that was abusive. I wanted to find that peace, and so I started to attend a church. I remember when a lady asked me if I knew Jesus. Yes, of course I knew of Him, but did I know Him? She prayed with me, and I wept as I turned my life over to Jesus and became born again. It was when I became a Christian that I found my worth and value did not hinge upon being given away, but on being adopted into the Kingdom of God. That void became filled, and I totally came to understand unconditional love.

I have also learned that grief is not something to fear or run from—it is how our hearts understand, process, heal, and mend. Perhaps certain losses will demand to be felt more than once, perhaps not. Twelve years ago, I lost my mother. She was my best friend, always there for me, and somehow always seemed to understand my journey of acceptance. Though she didn't carry me in her womb, she carried me in her arms and in her heart, and I continue to grieve the loss of my best friend.

On occasion, I think on the family I never got to know. The papers I found after my mom passed away tell that my birth mother was young and of average intelligence and that my father was handsome and reserved. These documents revealed so much I didn't know and yet such a miniscule amount of detail. There is asthma in my maternal family line, I was nineteen inches at birth, and my mother was actually of Scottish decent. But, these forms were filled out by the nurses at the hospital, they read impersonally, and they didn't answer any of the whys. I must admit, reading these words at points made me laugh and at points made me cry. Were they true, real, or a lame attempt at salvation of a weak, almost nonexistent memory?

My parents adopted my brother, too. As of lately, his biological mother has tried to contact him numerous times, and he would prefer if she didn't. Isn't it funny the outcomes we can't anticipate? We grew up in the same home, had the same upbringing, and yet I don't know who or where my parents are, while his have been knocking at his door for years. He doesn't want to meet this woman and that, I believe, is a fair choice. After all, she made choices that greatly affected him, and he could not do anything about it. I, however, wish I was also given that choice.

No doubt that often the sting of rejection burns when I realize that I am not being searched for, perhaps not even thought of. Granted, I only know how I feel. Maybe she has fought hard to find me and has come against a cold, hard wall. I won't ever know. I think at times, if I was given the choice, would I want to be found? My mom and dad were not perfect by any means—my mom often hid her true feeling of inadequacy, and my dad sometimes had a bad temper—but they were mine and I was theirs. Trying to conjure up in my mind an image of what my childhood could have been like has nothing on feeling my own mother's arms around me or watching her move around the kitchen.

There are pieces of my life I have lost, pieces I have only recently found, pieces I have always had, and pieces I may never know. In the Bible, Romans 8:28 reads that, "All things work together for the good of those who love The Lord," and I believe that truth stands firm in my life today. Would I have written my life story differently? Perhaps at one point I would have. Now? I believe that all things have worked together for my good. I am strong, I am proud of me, and most importantly, I know I am loved, cherished, and was handpicked from the beginning of my days for this incredible journey we call life.

Welcome Home
by Laureen Nowlan-Card

loved spending time with my grandmother. With her, I experienced the soothing balm of unconditional love. I felt completely loveable in her presence. Of course, I liked spending time with her at her house. Grammie's sparkling blue eyes would greet me at the front door, her warm hug enveloping my little body with love, and the smell of her—a mixture of Oil of Olay face cream and a bit of sweat from a day's hard work. It was a smell unique only to her, and to me, it smelled like home, belonging, and love.

Inside, I would be delighted to help her and my grandfather with the chores. Sometimes that would mean helping to set the table for dinner, straining the fresh cream off the cow milk, going to the chicken coop to collect eggs and water the hens, or—my favourite—going with her to pick raspberries for dessert.

Soon the rest of my family would arrive, my parents, siblings, uncles, aunts, and cousins. We'd all join together for dinner. Although the talk of politics and such could sometimes get a little heated, it was a lively and happy table most times.

It was after dinner that the feel of the house changed for me. That was when the grown-ups would talk all evening around the kitchen table, and the children would grow bored and rambunctious and be told to either go play in the living room or go outside to play. That's when the darkness that lived in my grandmother's house would come out.

He lurked in the shadows, waiting for me to be alone, and sometimes created situations to get me alone. I would grow anxious. The adults considered him a kid, but in his late teens, he was almost a man and every bit as strong as one. He would wrestle, tickle, and pick me up by my feet, hanging me upside down by my ankles, laughing. I would protest, my young brain trying to make up reasons that I could not play with him. No, I can't play hide-and-go-seek because he sometimes hid in the closet with me and touched me under my panties! I wish I had said that. As the opening song for the Sunday Disney movie played, he laid himself beside me and made me touch his bare penis under the big fuzzy blanket.

When I was five, I liked to pretend I was Snow White. I had long, black hair and pale, soft skin like her. Also like her, I loved playing in the forest next to my home, the little forest animals coming near me as I sat listening to the sounds of nature, feeling totally at home in this private world of mine. In that forest, I stumbled upon an old stone foundation of an ancient house. There were even some pieces of glassware and ceramic cups amongst the rubble overgrown with moss. The energy of this place was special. I could imagine the people who lived here, how they had lived in their "old fashioned" ways.

It was my special place, until one day he found me there. He snuck up on me. He laughed as he scared me to death with his big loud voice and his grabbing hands. I screamed and ran—over the moss, through the trees, branches whipping my face. Until he caught up to me. He was so much taller and faster. He snarled, "Stop screaming." Once caught, there was nothing I could do to resist. I was completely powerless when he decided to hang me by my ankles, to tickle me silly, to put me in a head lock, or to lie on top of me. When I did dare to struggle, he laughed at my completely futile efforts. I saw how that gave him even more satisfaction, and there was no way I was giving him that. So, when he laid his heavy body on top of me in the wet moss, I just lay there hoping it would end very soon.

I stopped going into the forest alone after that. I was afraid for my younger siblings to go into the woods alone too. Sometimes I had nightmares of being in the forest and not being able to find my way out.

A few months later, in late summer, the sun was shining, and the warm breeze was blowing across the tall grass at the back of my house, as the crickets chirped their summer song. I danced with the butterflies, ran through the hay, and lay down on my back, watching the clouds roll by. The tall grass shrouded me. My own little world. Peace.

Then I was up and running through the hay again when I saw him coming toward me. It was too late to run. He took me down over the hill where no one could see us. There in the grass, his body was heavy as he lay on top of me and tried to penetrate me. When he couldn't, he settled for between my legs. This wasn't new. He'd done this before, in his room, in the closet, on the couch. What I remember most about these times is his heavy panting breath and him telling me that he'd "get me" if I told anyone.

At some point growing up, I learned that when you've been abused, you are damaged or broken in some way. This didn't seem right to me—I didn't feel damaged or broken. I was fine. I was better than fine—I was smart, pretty, kind, and a good girl. I didn't talk about what he did, because I felt that admitting what had happened to me would be admitting that I was broken and damaged.

I spent most of the next thirty-five years proving to myself and the outside world that I was not broken or damaged. Becoming a master chameleon, I adapted myself to be what pleased others. I became an overachiever, driven by the hidden fear of being "not good enough" or "broken." My achievements were a signal to the outside world of my worthiness and a reaffirmation to myself that I was good enough. Straight As, being the "nicest," making sure everyone was pleased with me. Writing contests, public speaking contests, lead in the band and school plays. Volunteering for every club in high school, graduating high school with honours and scholarships while working a part-time job. Honour roll and more awards in undergraduate and law school.

As soon as I achieved a goal, I moved on to the next without even celebrating the achievement. For example, I didn't even go to my law school graduation. I had already moved on to my coveted first job as a crown prosecutor.

Through this work, for over twenty years, I have done my best to show compassion for victims of crime as well as perpetrators. As a result of my own experiences, I have been able to relate to victims of abuse and have helped hundreds of women and children navigate the criminal justice process. I believe that I have touched many lives in a positive way.

At work, I continued overworking and trying for perfection. Except, in the real world, perfection is rarely attainable and there is a never-ending workload. Add to that a couple of children and the overwhelming urge to be a "perfect" mother to my precious ones, and I was a burnout waiting to happen. My self-care was nonexistent. I expected myself to push through everything.

After so many years of looking outside myself for approval, I had forgotten how to listen inwardly, except for my inner critic who was plenty loud. I had stopped listening to my body so long ago that when a life coach suggested I listen to my body, I exclaimed, "What? My body? If I listen to my body, it will have nothing good to say because I just use my body to get my brain from one place to another!"

During my pregnancies, I worked until the day before my children were born. I literally went from court, to being in labour, and then home with my babies.

As you might imagine, this led to complete depletion after my second child was born. Post-partum depression was my breakdown and the beginning of my personal transformation. I didn't really accept that I was in a depression for the first six months, but when my depression got to the point that my brain couldn't function anymore, I knew I needed help. I felt like I was trapped in a wet paper bag and I couldn't get out.

Antidepressants rebalanced my brain chemistry so I could function again. Then began the task of relearning how to live life. Even though I had done lots of self-help work before the depression, I hadn't really changed how I was living. I realized that no matter how fast I ran, I could not outrun my fears, wounds, or emotions. It was time to stop and heal.

I sought resources to relearn how to live in a way that was sustainable. After all, life is not a sprint; it's a marathon. I began counseling and learned cognitive behaviour methods. Seeking connection with other women, I participated in women's groups focused on finding more joy in life. I began yoga and Pilates classes for both the physical and the meditative benefits. I had never heard of Kundalini Yoga, but I loved it from the first class. The movements, the meditative chanting, and the philosophy were so transformational that I credit it with saving me. Kundalini Yoga continues to be a key practice in my life to this day. I have deepened my practice to include emotional liberation methods that help me understand and honour my highly sensitive, emotional nature and to use my emotions as guides to live with more joy and peace.

The next level in my healing came when I trained to become a transformational life coach. I learned about and worked on limiting beliefs—things I came to believe about myself and the world as a result of things that happened to me before I was six years old. I learned about emotional triggers and how they relate to past traumas. With these tools, I was able to release my old beliefs and manage my triggers so that I can live an empowered life where I am no longer in reaction mode.

I found myself drawn to women's circles and ancient goddess ways. It was in these circles of deep, wholehearted women that I realized how much I had turned away from the feminine and abandoned entire parts of myself. The little girl who frolicked so joyfully in the forest and fields, who loved all things and herself, began to whisper to me that she was still with me. Slowly, she began to emerge and, eventually, a great reunion occurred.

As I healed myself, I also wanted to reach out and help others. I saw the women around me, in all walks of life, running themselves ragged, ignoring their desires and needs, traumatized and triggered, giving up parts of themselves, and really having no idea how amazing they were. I knew their struggle, and, thanks to my journey, I also knew how to help.

Thanks to my studies as a life coach and emotional guide, I now have the privilege of helping other women release themselves from the shackles of their pasts and embody their highest selves. I now coach women to stop running on the emotional avoidance treadmill, stop over giving, stop people pleasing, and stop hiding parts of themselves. When a woman is released from the bondage of her past limiting beliefs, she comes home to her pure potential, wholeness, and freedom. I've been incredibly privileged to say "welcome home" to many women. This has been the gift arising out of my journey.

As I healed my wounds, released my fears and limiting beliefs, and learned to love all parts of myself again, I have come home to my true and whole self. A few summers ago, I went back to the farm, and I walked through the forest alone, skipped through the fields, picked flowers, and danced with butterflies. I felt my very real connection to nature and the world around me. I cried for the little girl who lost so much of herself there, and I showed her that it was safe for her to be seen and to be her loving self. Soon my tears of sadness turned to tears of joy as I reunited with those playful, imaginative, feminine, trusting, and joyful parts of myself. My journey had finally brought me to wholeness again. Standing in the sunlit field, I whispered, "Welcome home, I'm so happy you're here."

A Pastor, a Prayer, and a Miracle
by Jennifer Strachan

I am an addict in recovery. My name is Jennifer. I struggled speaking those words for many years as I didn't believe them to be true. I had judgements as to what a real drug addict looked like, I was in denial and rationalized that I wasn't that bad.

After watching me abuse drugs for over ten years, my younger sister staged an intervention. I was forty-five years old, unhappily married, and thought I had done a great job at hiding my using. My jig was about to be up.

The day my sister showed up at my house, confronted me with the truth, and offered me help, I ran upstairs yelling for her to "get the f@$% out of my house." I slammed my bedroom door, sat on my bed, and broke down in tears.

Anxious and fearful, I knew I was no longer going to be able to hide behind the masks or the lies. My biggest worry was having my son taken away from me.

I knew I had two choices—I could continue to slowly kill myself and lose my son, or I could accept my sister's help and attend a treatment program, knowing I would have to give up a long term, intimate relationship with my best friends: alcohol and drugs.

After wiping my tears, I emerged from my room and agreed to accept the help for my drug problem, while secretly hoping that I might be able to learn how to moderate my alcohol consumption. The thought of never ever having another drink terrified me, and so did facing the consequences of my behaviour.

A few days later, my sister picked me up to take me to rehab. I waved goodbye to a disgraced husband and my twelve-year-old son.

Few words were spoken on our three-hour drive, but my shitty committee, however, spoke loud and clear.

Some people called me courageous for agreeing to go, but I felt like a coward, and the negative self-talk I lived with confirmed this.

For as long as I can remember, I've had voices in my head that berate me, telling me that I'm fat, stupid, ugly, can't do anything right, no one will ever love me, that I'm worthless, a bad mom, and that I don't deserve anything good in life.

Today I refer to these voices as the "shitty committee." They are the imaginary bat I beat myself up with, the hurtful words that play over and over again in my head like a broken record. This was my soundtrack on the way to rehab.

Upon arrival at the facility, my sister and I were greeted by a woman who identified herself as a counselor, and she gave us a tour. Our first stop was the common area, which had an old brown couch, matching loveseat, and a beat-up coffee table with a deck of cards and a crib board neatly stacked in the middle.

We were then escorted through the TV room of the women's dorm. Several clients stared at me, I'm sure wondering who I was. We continued walking down a hallway to my room, where the counselor inspected my luggage for contraband, which I didn't have. She then suggested I make myself at home and left me and my sister to unpack my bags.

My room smelled like mothballs. It had two single bed frames attached to the walls across from one another, a small desk, a red plastic chair, and an alarm clock. I remember thinking, "what a dump."

The pillows and bunk-style mattresses were flat and lumpy with a flimsy comforter and sheets that didn't match. How the hell did I end up in this place? I didn't belong here.

I had my own business and owned a nice car. I had never been arrested, and I wasn't putting a needle in my arm or drinking out of a brown paper bag behind a dumpster; I was better than that and definitely better than this.

Upon further inspection of my accommodations, I found a shared washroom, several mouse traps throughout the building, and ragged carpets and windows that were covered with plastic-lined curtains.

I was so busy judging and picking apart my home for the next six weeks that I hadn't even noticed the serene ranch environment around me—flowing meadows, beautiful evergreen trees, and wildflowers growing in abundance.

After giving me a hug and a few words of encouragement, my sister left. At a much later date, she admitted that she was reluctant to leave me there.

But then, I found myself alone again and wondering what was in store for me at this twelve-step treatment facility. I knew the twelve steps had something to do with God. I, however, had abandoned God in my teens and hadn't had a relationship with him in over twenty-five years. The God I grew up with was unforgiving and punishing, unless I spoke three Hail Marys after attending confession for my sins.

As a teenager, I remember feeling rebellious one afternoon and decided not to recite these prayers, to see whether lightning would strike me down on the steps of the church. I survived that afternoon and thought maybe God had instead destined me for hell.

The morning after I arrived for treatment, I attended my first coaching class. I remember several takeaways from the teachings: I had a disease that I was not responsible for having, but I was responsible for my recovery.

I was told to keep no secrets, and that my problem was not drugs; my problem was actually me.

I remember feeling quite disgusted at such an accusation. My nose went out of joint and my posture went straight up in defense. What do you mean my problem was me? How could my problem possibly be me? I had blamed everyone *but* me.

In a small group, we started working the twelve steps of recovery. I was able to admit that I was powerless and that my life had become unmanageable. I struggled, however, with a power greater than myself—the God thing scared me. I didn't trust God, and God didn't love me.

I had a counselor who told me if the God of my understanding wasn't working for me today, I could fire his ass and get a new one.

Whoa! That concept blew my mind open. I didn't know that I could believe in something different, like a loving, forgiving, and beautiful God.

My counselor suggested that I pray, but I hadn't yet gotten to know and trust this new concept of God. How could I pray to something I didn't believe in?

I thought maybe I could use an angel for strength and guidance instead, so I started praying to my mom, who died of brain cancer several years before I walked through the doors of rehab.

Days after Mom's terminal diagnosis, I had quit my job to be her full-time caregiver. Her last days turned into months, and I watched her deteriorate, losing her beautiful blonde hair, weight, and appetite. I couldn't bring myself to talk to her about dying, and I didn't want her to see I was falling apart.

I went from frequently getting loaded to getting loaded all day, every day. I had become so accustomed to numbing pain and avoiding feelings that I lost my ability to believe I was strong enough without the use of drugs to face the demons that haunted me.

Now, while in rehab, I was overwhelmed with many painful memories, many of which kept me awake at night. Unable to sleep, I would meander into the TV room to spend time with the night shift crew, with whom I was growing a friendship. I will always remember Dawn—she was loving, kind, and compassionate. Her alternate shift worker was Diane, a newly hired member of the women's support team. Little did I know, God was placing these women as angels on my path!

On my journey of healing trauma, grief, pain, and loss, I continued to pray. I didn't know whether or not I would ever be able to forgive myself for some of the things I had done. I was drowning in feelings of guilt, shame, and remorse, with very few coping skills.

After three weeks of getting to know a new God while working steps two and three, I asked him to help me. In return, I said I would surrender to him all my broken pieces, including all my secrets. I believe it was these prayers that gave me the courage and strength to walk through my web of dishonesty, denial, and painful truths.

The time came for me to write step four—revealing unhealed events that were over a decade old, years before the death of my mom. Back then, my police officer husband was poked by a positive HIV, hepatitis C needle, while arresting a drug addict. When I got the news, I quickly found care for our eighteen-month-old son and rushed to emergency. I entered through the automatic glass doors and was escorted past the prisoner's holding cell. A small window in the door allowed me to see inside, to see the man responsible for our life-changing moment. His clothing was ripped, and he was covered in blood and handcuffed to the wall.

With contempt and hatred, I glared at him.

I walked away and into the room where my husband was being treated, and the doctors decided to prescribe a concoction of antiviral medication. We were told the risk was small for transfer, but we were to use condoms and not to conceive a baby until he was cleared of being at risk.

When we got home the next morning, my husband decided he wanted to be abstinent. He told me I was free to do what I needed to as a sexual woman; he simply didn't want to know about it. I wasn't thinking about what he must've been going through. I was unhappily married and had been given permission to go outside of my marriage. So that's what I selfishly did.

During that time, my husband and I stopped kissing, hugging, holding hands, and laughing; we stopped being friends. A year passed, and he tested negative for HIV and hepatitis C.

After one last sexual encounter, I ended the affair I'd been having, and I put forth an effort into saving our failing marriage. Even after pressuring my husband to attend marital counseling, I was still unable to be honest.

I discovered I was pregnant and desperately tried to calculate the date of conception. I wasn't able to process the small possibility that my husband wasn't the father, and I knew our marriage wasn't stable enough to bring a new baby into this world. I prayed to God that he would terminate my pregnancy with a miscarriage.

Hating myself and my life, I punched my abdomen, ran into the corner of my bathroom counter, and fell to the ground and wept.

Two months later, I went to my first ultrasound. While my husband sat in the waiting room, the technician moved the machine over my visibly pregnant belly. She spent five silent minutes with me and then asked me to wait for the doctor, who would be in shortly.

I already knew what he was going to tell me when he came in to deliver the news that my baby didn't have a heartbeat.

A nurse brought my husband into the examination room, and we looked at the frozen image on the screen. As we hugged each other and cried, my tears were full of the inconceivable thought that I was responsible for the death of my baby.

Why didn't I miscarry? I believed God wanted me to suffer—to go through the painful feelings, to carry around a dead baby for over twenty-four hours, to endure the mental torture of a medical abortion as I waited for my baby's body to be removed from mine.

When my husband drove me to the hospital for the procedure, I remember feeling numb and robotic. I was given a cubical, a gown, and paperwork to fill out. After my husband left, I was given a sedative and wheeled into a cold room with a large overhead light. The last thing I remember was my ankles being shackled apart.

I woke up to a woman asking me if I wanted to name my baby girl and have a funeral for her. I replied with a cold, "No," and asked her to leave.

My husband picked me up and we drove home in silence. As with anything else difficult or painful in our lives, we never spoke of our loss.

It was time for me to share my step five: "We admitted to God, to ourselves, and to another human being the exact nature of our wrongs."

Across the parking lot of the treatment center, I met with a minister underneath a beautiful tree whose branches provided shade. I sat in a lawn chair across from him, and he held my hands as I surrendered the darkest parts of me.

My voice was shaky, and my head hung low, and I cried as I shared things I had done. My feelings of guilt and shame were overwhelming and so painful to admit. I felt responsible for the death of my daughter.

This minister looked me in the eyes and told me how much God loved me and that I was forgiven.

I stood up and thanked him. As I walked back through the gravel parking lot to the center, I desperately wanted to believe that what he said was true. I felt exposed and vulnerable.

On my way, I happened to see Diane from the night shift walking to the office. I asked her what she was doing there, and she said that she was picking up her paycheck and was on her way to see her daughter, who had just given birth to a baby girl.

I could feel her excitement. I gave her a big hug and asked her the name of her granddaughter. Diane said the baby's name was Jennifer Marie.

My first name is Jennifer. My middle name is Marie.

I felt the hand of God touch me. Goosebumps covered me from head to toe, and my eyes swelled with happy tears. Somehow, this baby's birth opened my heart, allowing the light to start shining from within.

In that moment, I knew the grace of God. I surrendered and had experienced a spiritual awakening along with the miracle of another day free from active addiction. I began a whole new relationship with God and with myself.

Eventuality of Flight
by Sheryl Rist

Those who believe in many lives and supposedly have the gift of psychic ability tell me that this is my last time here on earth. Perhaps they're right. It's also possible that I am preparing to be a guide for those yet to come. Maybe that's why I am in service. I don't know. I kind of want to come around again and live the perfect life of a happy marriage with 2.5 kids, a white-picket fence around the mansion, and fancy cars to drive along sunny, warm, winding beach roads, on my way to my surfboard and yacht. That has not been this lifetime, at least not yet. But then, how can I know anything as solid fact when so much of life involves perception, time, choices, and differing points of view? I used to believe a simple spoon was solid and unchangeable by the mind. Then I met a woman who could bend spoons with her mind. So, what is real? What is possible?

My mom tried to teach me what she could as I was growing up. Her wisdom was as wide as a river with rapids that I had to course through. She tried to teach me that possibilities were available if you searched, yet frequently, she didn't believe in possibilities in her own life or the world. "Time heals everything," she would say. Having lost my mom recently and, feeling the overwhelming confusion and sadness that accompanies her absence, I have my doubts about this. Deep down, I know that time eases the pain in the heart so it's not a stabbing agony every second of every day, but I also know that I must still put the work in to heal wounds and traumas.

Mom didn't believe in the possibility of healing wounds and trauma. She believed that you just had to suck it up and continue on with life. Perhaps this is the way she lived life in her own mind. I know from experience, both professional and personal, that if you do not heal a wound, it festers and eventually affects everything. To an unhealed wound, even simple things like a gentle friendly hug or words of encouragement can appear as groping or slander. I've learned that it's necessary to heal wounds so that my sight and understanding are clear, and so I can see more possibilities for myself than just wounding.

"Perception is everything," Mom would say. While I agree that adjusting perception can be important, in some circumstances, fact trumps perception. A seven-year-old girl who is molested does not care about perception. She cares that she has been violated and life is never the same again. She requires the support and comfort of those around her to help organize and sort through the jumble of thoughts in her young mind. To gently lead her by the hand to an understanding and a life as free as possible from the impact.

That seven-year-old girl was me—molested by a great uncle who was my babysitter for a summer, at least until I saw the possibility of courage. Courage to stand up for myself and say to him, "No more. That is enough. Go away!" I am proud of that beautiful soul and see the courage that has always been within her.

Although I said no to my abuser, I told no one else what happened, and even though I was hurt inside from the abuse, I lived on. As a child, I felt I had been born with wings that soared along the lines of possibilities, and nothing could stop me. Of course, these wings were only in my imagination. I went through my childhood always aware of what was going on around me, yet able to daydream myself into soothing flight to avoid reality. Thankfully, my imagination was fruitful, and I had learned the possibilities that emerged when I stood up for myself and trusted my instincts. Once, a teenage boy tried to kiss me when I was nine, two years after I had stood up to my great uncle. This time, right away, I simply placed my hands on my hips and forcefully told this boy what he could do with that request.

Eventually, I became a teenager. I smoked, did gentle drugs, and drank alcohol, but never really got into trouble. I thought I was tough enough to stop all the monsters of life. Boy, was I wrong.

During high school, I started to date and become involved in romantic relationships. Everything always started out great and then ended in difficulty and confusion for me. I was not ready for sexual contact, and it always left me feeling yucky and frantic inside. The boys I dated would affect my heart and mind in ways unseen by my friends and parents. As my friends had none of the same problems, I questioned my feelings. I now realize this was a result of the sexual abuse I experienced as a child. My inability to function in a sexual relationship would frustrate my dates, and the outcomes of this frustration were unpredictable and often hurtful to me.

I wanted to believe that life was better than this, that I didn't come here for this. I wanted the beauty I saw in the sky and trees and flowers. I could see beauty all around me to such great extents that I believed every human soul to be the same. Many times, I was wrong, as all souls are on a journey of their own, and some journeys are not pleasant.

Like others who have been abused as children, I blocked out the sexual trauma only to revisit it photographically in my mind when I was in my twenties. At twenty years old, I finally told my mom what happened that summer. Mom did not see the courage, and instead insisted that almost all women go through sexual abuse as children. She told me not to make such a big deal out of it and get on with life. She said my perception of the situation would change as I became older. To her, there was nothing to heal and no other approach necessary. I wasn't sure what to think, but part of me knew she was wrong.

I am still grateful for a local Support, Education, and Prevention of Sexual Abuse (SEPSA) group, which allowed me to be part of the healing it offered. At our weekly meetings, kind and skilled facilitators taught our group healthy ways to process our anger and simple exercises to cultivate self-love.

After a year in the group, I thought I was finally free of trauma and was looking forward to romantic relationships. I desperately wanted to take flight in this way, and little did I know that I wasn't ready yet. I repeated the same pattern over and over again. Romantic relationships became a side stream in my life, fraught with midnight black horses of doom tumbling through the atmosphere and grazing my fluttering wings. It was not yet safe for me to fly in these air currents. I did not realize that I had only gone through the first level of healing and had much more to learn and other possibilities to experience.

After each relationship, I would take time to recharge. Normally, this would involve years of celibacy and soul searching. I started to watch the greats—Deepak Chopra, Buddha, Gandhi, Mother Teresa, and Princess Diana. People I could look up to. People who were wise and had great thoughts to share. I ended up training with a female native shaman, and I spent years with her, learning and expanding my soul. Chanting, yoga, and walking meditation were all powerful friends. I could sweat with the best of them and had many experiences with different native tribes. And I could heal—deeply and soundly with more wisdom and in more ways than I had previously experienced. I learned about herbs, oils, foods, naturopathy, and acupuncture, how each of these modalities helped different conditions, and how to use them.

Then, after four to eight years, I would set out, seeking the companionship of romance again. I knew I had to keep up with my spiritual practices or things would go wrong. And when I didn't, things did go wrong. Looking back now, it is obvious what my big life learnings were and are: stay true to self and practices; do not get wrapped up in the romance and give all of self and all of self-power away. Yet since I was still learning, each time I would fall head over heels and give up my all. Here I am, I'd say in more ways than one, please do with me as you wish.

While selfless giving can seem or be seen like an honorable way to be connected with other humans, it doesn't make for healthy or successful relationships. Boundaries are necessary for care and sustainability of self. Each time things went wrong in relationship, I experienced more trauma, and my body became tired. So, I had to step away. It was imperative that I stay healthy to be active and vibrant. That was who I was and wanted to be. So even though I prayed for a successful relationship, that possibility was not realistic. I needed to learn love, boundaries, self-care, and myself.

Life for me has been a consistent journey through trauma to the other side. It has been about learning boundaries that incorporate self-love. It has been about imagining new possibilities and strengthening my wings to fly toward these possibilities. Each step, each possibility has brought me closer to healing the trauma within my soul. Herbs, yoga, acupuncture, hypnosis, and sweats have been a few of the important steps. Only through the love and care that I have given myself, have I healed.

Now after thirty years of repeating unhealthy relationship patterns, I feel I have finally stopped the patterns and cleared the mind and trauma from my body. I have come to a place where I am grateful for all that I have been through. Strange, maybe, but necessary. My soul is more open than ever before. I love with each breath, and that love has become me. Because I have become love, it is very easy to share it. I breathe in, and I breathe out. I love in, and I love out. I did not just feel compassion; I became it. I became boundaries instead of being caged within them. I have learned to care for myself in ways that I wish to share. With almost two decades as an acupuncturist and doctor of natural medicine, I have the honor and privilege of sharing these learnings daily with those who see me. I live a life of joy, gratitude, understanding, courage, and most of all, love.

Some of the ways that I care for myself are those that many speak about—meditation, yoga, walking, speaking, journaling, herbs, minerals, vitamins, etc. Some I am good at, and some I am quite terrible at. I am not good at sitting meditation; I like to move around. My favorite activity is meditating yoga. It is possible to cleanse the energy from the mind and body while moving, and this practice is powerful and time friendly.

My shamanic teacher said my specialty was walking meditation. I could walk and hear all around me. The birds always had stories to tell, and their singing brought me deep comfort. I could figure out my world during a walk. My favorite walks are always near water, and in the summer, I love walking near the river where I live. The summer sun warms my soul while the water washes away the emotional and mental daily grit.

Just recently on one of my walks, I realized the extent to which energy can become trapped in the body due to trauma. I believe the energy increases with each trauma experienced until it results in disease. The trauma can be sexual, physical, or emotional and will affect the cells of the body. After a trauma, the body retains the shock, negative energy, and karmic print upon it. For instance, I experienced very serious bowel problems during my teenage years and realized that childhood trauma was the cause of it. Through the use of herbs, naturopathy, and acupuncture, I was able to resolve this condition. I find with patients that if the trauma can be recognized and healed, the body will also heal itself of diseases.

The body, and the trauma that can build up within it, can be healed through many different modalities and practices. First, the energy built up from traumas must be released from the body through physical exercise, and I love yoga and walking meditation for this purpose. I believe the body may also be supplemented to support this energetic cleanse and recommend the use of natural vitamins, supplements, oils, and food to help heal myself and others. I am so thankful for natural medicine as it compliments my beliefs and values. I feel it's important to see the body as a holistic machine. Like a machine, it requires its own kind of oil, gas, and transmission fluid to run properly.

It is impossible to spread my wings out fully if the feathers are dull and falling out from lack of nourishment. It is impossible to fly if my bones are poorly arranged due to lack of energetic flow. It is impossible to soar if my mind is unable to focus due to congestion of traumatic thoughts within. Clear the mind, clear the energy, nourish the body, and strengthen the soul. This is the way to fly toward the possibilities. And courage—the most important ingredient of all.

Without courage, it was not possible for me to take the steps necessary to untangle from the darkness of the trauma. Without courage, I could not start on a nutritional plan to strengthen and support myself. Courage for boundaries, courage to stand tall, courage to exercise, courage to love myself. Without courage, I would not have said no to my abuser at the age of seven. Without courage, I would not have become an acupuncturist. Without courage, I would not be writing this story. Without courage and an openness to what's possible, my life would be very different.

As is normal, a few times during my journey, I was so tired that I had no courage left. I didn't know what to do. I forgot how to heal. So, I reached out to a support network, and that was the first step in remembering. Once I reached out, friends seemed to step forward at just the right time, encouraging me with their words, helping me with daily activities, going for walks with me. With their love, they lifted me above the ruckus, so I could stand again. I started to take supplements and feed myself healthy foods that I had researched. I found things to be grateful for—being alive, the trees and the birds, the sun rising daily. I remembered to love myself more than anything else. To stand for myself and take time for myself.

I remembered that healing was possible, that I was possible. I remembered little Sheryl. She was brave and would ride her pony until dark. She wasn't afraid of anything. She was strong and mighty and knew how to say no. She also knew that she had wings and held tight to the promise that, for a creature born with wings, one thing was certain: the eventuality of flight.

Living With the Hand I Was Dealt
by Kurtis Clay

I don't suffer with Asperger's syndrome. I live with it. Not to say it doesn't feel like suffering at times. The hard part is not understanding why I feel and act like I do, but getting people to realize I don't do things on purpose. It's just the way my brain is wired. I have never known anything else, and it is like being born without one limb. You adapt to the situation.

It's difficult for me to tell an original story. For me, it's easier to recite someone else's creation because I have a photographic memory, or to make lists and give examples. For my voicing career, I can mimic other voices I have heard, and find it easy to recreate the exact sound. So, on that note, here is my list of things that I live with while doing life with Asperger's:

- I have difficulty looking people in the eye. It is uncomfortable for me and causes me to feel panicked. In other words: fight or flight. This happens quite often, and I can't help feeling confronted in most conversations, even though it's usually something that has zero confrontation behind it. If I look at people, I'm trying to determine what their mood is (which, in itself, is difficult), and I can't focus on what they're saying. A little technique my parents taught me: look at the person's cheek, in that way, it looks like you're making eye contact, but I can still focus on what they're saying, and not appear rude.
- There are certain fabrics that become instantly unbearable to wear, and I want to take it off immediately. Even if an undershirt is placed beneath the offending one, I still find it unbearably itchy. It's hard to explain because

it feels itchy, but it's not. The clothing is so distracting that I can't focus on anything but being shed of that garment. Labels in the backs of clothing are awful too. It was a day of jubilation when most manufacturers started printing the labels onto the fabric instead of attaching a tag. The type of clothing I absolutely can't wear are sweaters.

- I am prone to having emotional outbursts. When a situation arises, I feel a lack of control over it, and my mind thinks an outburst will make it easier for me to cope. Typically, my outbursts happen in a game when I'm playing it. I'm not the small Italian plumber in the fictional game. So, I can't control him, only limited by the game's controls. It's silly, but this lack of control drives me crazy.

- Some foods are inedible to me. For me to eat, the texture must feel "right." I have an aversion to a bitter sensation, and if I even entertain the idea of a vegetable, it cannot be cooked. Steamed vegetables are the worst for me. Every time I try to eat one, especially if it's green beans, and even coleslaw, I gag every time. Stir fried, sautéed, or fried vegetables are fine, however.

- I live with an inner frustration of not feeling quite "right," and not knowing how to fix it.

- Awkward movements, such as stimming, is a repetitive body movement that helps me self-stimulate, and bring my sense of well-being under control. I also have the tendency to pace, which is also a self-regulating technique for me. I use one of the fidget cubes to play around with. Other stimming activities include organizing my collector's cards and making lists.

- I struggle with seemingly simple tasks and must have step-by-step instructions for a number of times before I am comfortable completing the tasks on my own.

- I have little to no patience. If something doesn't work out, or is taking longer than I like, I give up quickly.

- I have a big issue with believing my self-worth to this world. People who live with Asperger's have a negative outlook on almost everything, and never think we are good enough for anything. Depression also is a key factor for us Aspies.

- Sounds that I have no control over are excruciatingly unbearable. But, if I control the volume, the sound can blow the roof off a house and it wouldn't bother me. Usually higher pitched noises bother me. Especially our house alarm. I take special precautions to make sure I always deactivate it before entering the house. Otherwise, that noise will invade my ears. Another sound I can't tolerate is children in restaurants, airplanes, or other enclosed places.

- Certain smells, even ones that smell good to others, can be repulsive, or even unbearable to me. Vinegar is the strongest example of this. It smells utterly awful to me.

- I have a lack of motivation. I don't want to do anything that involves too much time or effort, unless it is something that I really want to do.

- To be brutally honest, I hate my looks, and everything about myself. Low self-esteem is my friend.

- Although my voice and all the great things I can do with it is my career, I hate it. Low self-esteem at its finest.

- I am constantly self-conscious of everything I'm involved in. I don't like drawing attention to myself, but with Asperger's and all my peculiarities, that's exactly what happens.

- When I get involved in something I'm extremely interested in, I "zone out." The apocalypse could be happening around me, and I would have no clue. Hard to explain, but, for some reason, my mind tends to tune out because I either focus too hard or get distracted. While in my basement recording studio, it is beneficial to have this focus because I am not distracted by outside influences when my headphones are on, and voicing is the subject at hand.

- I get involved with certain interests, and it becomes an obsession. If it is collecting items for a set, I feel the need to have one of each.

- Someone may be attempting to have a conversation with me, but if I'm "into" one of my interests, I will pay no attention to what you're saying, have a one-track mind, and talk over you.

- I have awkward speech patterns and repeat things.

- I take things literally: if my mom said she was going to "pinch my head off" or "jerk a knot in my tail," I think that's what is going to happen. I have learned to ask if she's kidding so that I don't waste precious time wondering. Of course, she laughs, and then, that's my cue that this is something humorous.

- I must have a structured day. I need to know in what order things are happening and at what time. Don't tell me a certain time for anything unless it will happen exactly at that time. I have to be told that an "unexpected" may happen, or I will go into defense mode and shut down. I do everything, almost every day, at the same time. Things like taking a shower, brushing my teeth, and eating are scheduled.

Asperger's syndrome is not a yoke around my neck that prevents me from living. In most ways, it enhances my abilities. For years, I tried to use it as an excuse for my actions, which was not allowed by my parents. I learned that I should embrace my uniqueness and accept this as a gift. I live with Asperger's. I don't suffer with it.

Surely Rising
by Kit Fraser

An old man once lured me to his trailer, tempting me with the promise of cookies and milk. His grandson, Jimmy, and I often played together in a big field of tall, dense weeds beside the mobile-home park or down into the gully behind, and I thought that Jimmy would be there enjoying cookies, too. I knew the old guy, so I accepted his invitation and happily skipped along, my little child mind intent on the cookies.

Inside, the surroundings seemed quite dark once I realized that Jimmy wasn't there. No one else was there. I remember seeing a big hazy open room with streaks of sunlight squishing through some cracks in the thick, droopy curtains, and the kitchen in which we stood had an island counter-top skirted by tall metal stools.

As I looked about wondering where everybody was, the old man suddenly scooped me up and plopped himself onto a stool with me on his lap.

"Let me down!" I exclaimed, struggling intently to free myself from his grasp. "Where's Jimmy?"

"Don't worry, Jimmy will be here in a minute," he said huskily, tightening his grip around my waist. Then, without warning, he shoveled a hand under my clothing between my legs, his fat, rough fingers rudely prodding into my private parts.

My mind was racing as I panicked in a chaotic whirl of horror. I had to get free!

"What's wrong?" he asked, adding, "My grandkids like this. It's okay."

"I have to go to the bathroom!" I blurted.

Holding firm, he shushed me, seeming astonished at my distress.

I kept insisting and struggling, so he finally withdrew his hand and slid me down the chair's metal leg, dropping me to the floor. "Go to the bathroom in the hallway," he said gruffly, sounding annoyed.

I retorted, "My mom says I have to go home when I need to go to the bathroom!" and kept backing slowly toward the doorway in the hall between the old man and the bathroom.

"No, no, she won't mind just this once. Stay here," he said.

By then, I was at the doorway, and seizing my escape, I bolted from the trailer out into the bright sunlight, running as fast as my legs would carry me. He didn't chase me.

Once home, I know that I quickly informed my stepmom of at least part of the incident, and she relayed many years later in conversation that Dad had somehow addressed that dirty old man for abusing his six-year-old girl.

Grade one found me rejected by the school's teaching faculty. Apparently, my poor speech was alarming, and I didn't respond or pay attention, so was therefore considered retarded. They didn't think normal grade school was appropriate for me. After a myriad of medical tests, it was discovered that I was unable to hear sounds above a certain frequency, including those forming the basics of language.

My parents chose not to follow the system that would have put me in a special school. Instead, with the use of phonetic tools, my stepmom of three years began the long process of personally teaching me how to articulate words. Challenged hearing was both a curse and my savior, often evoking ridicule and judgement from bullies young and old, while rousing uplifting praise and special guidance from people more aware.

When I was ten, my family uprooted, moving hundreds of miles from my childhood friends. At our new home in BC's interior, we lived beside a lake far away from town, and there were no longer children close by to play with. My brother, who was seven years older than me, moved away to his own life.

Focusing on a routine of school and music, I would arise each school-day morning to practice piano before venturing the mile-long road to the highway bus stop. I composed my earliest piano music during those first years by the lake. This piece was suitably entitled "Far Away" as I mourned in my loneliness, missing my friends. Still, I was gifted with an awesome playmate who my parents would bring from town occasionally. His dad and mine were buddies, and we remain good friends.

Strangely perceptive, I could always feel the presence of nonphysical entities. As these sensations grew stronger, my dread was devouring, yet I fearfully concealed my terror. Countless nights found me awake, anticipating a scraping sound on the wall, or my closet door mysteriously swaying on its own. Sometimes my bed would shake, and I'd feel a sensation of nothingness eerily touching my body.

As I lay there in trepidation, trying to hide from the dark, my mind would ask questions. Who am I? What is our world inside of? To me, everything was contained within something else, and I would wander in my thoughts to the outermost regions of an imagined universe, seeking peace.

My teenage years were fraught with secrecy in so many ways. Abusively tarnished into an unhealthy physical awareness far too early, my inquisitive mind became sexually warped. I also seemed to be a magnet for guys of unhealthy morality, including an older man that owned a bakery beside the highway bus stop. For a few years, he had gained my trust by providing kindness and friendship, inviting me to wait inside on cold or rainy days. I was devastated that morning when he molested me in the bakery, and I never allowed myself to be alone with him again.

At fifteen years of age, I gathered some personal belongings into a green garbage bag and climbed out my bedroom window. Sneaking quietly into the dark, cold forest in the middle of winter, I trudged through knee-deep snow, trying to remain undetected. It was a week and more of surviving on my own, scrounging for dinner leftovers from friends sworn to secrecy, eating rancid food, sleeping on stranger's dirty floors without pillow or blanket, and existing in a manner I wasn't accustomed to. Finally, I arrived on my biological mother's Alberta doorstep, mentally destroyed and sick with pneumonia.

My brother and I had been separated from our mother when I was one, due to a very unhappy divorce. We then lived with our paternal grandparents, seeing our mom occasionally, until Dad remarried when I was three and moved us far away.

Now, Mom and her new fiancé lived in Calgary with my little sister, renting a temporary home as they joined together in life. They welcomed me kindly, and I felt very excited to get to know the mother that I had always silently yearned for.

I remember Mom and me standing in the kitchen one day shortly after my arrival, cautiously whispering about the dark shadow that had just glided past our line of sight. Mom had heard banging under the kitchen floor a few days prior, while in the house alone. She described the sound as someone striking a broom handle on the ceiling below her. Leaving her dishes, she went down to investigate, finding nothing and no one. There was something disturbingly unnatural in the house, and we were feeling it.

Other than babyhood, I had met my mom's brother only once during a preteen visit to meet my birth mother. An incredibly creepy man, seven years older than me, he visited regularly in this haunted house, fervently celebrating the sinister energy.

Along with finally getting to know my little sister, I also felt blessed to build a friendship with the daughter of my mom's fiancé. She would visit often, and since we shared the same age, we also shared the basement room. For a while, we were very close, and I still think of her as my sister.

Slowly but surely, we all became preoccupied with the ghostly events around us. There were chilling apparitions and bizarre occurrences throughout the house. In my room, the face on a hanging wall poster would distort with a menacing snarl; and one horrible evening, an impossible manifestation of blood dripping claw marks raked heavily down my sister's back as she sat in a recliner. The entities were menacing.

We became deeply ensnared within an ethereal spider web of sticky, penetrating fear. Shadows seemed to be lurking behind each corner, in every single glance, and with my natural inclination to feel the otherworld, I was totally obsessed with the nightmare around me.

My uncle was also overcome, but his response was not one of fear. It was more opportunistic. He relentlessly preyed on my mind, saying that I had become possessed, insisting that he needed to reach a deep-rooted chakra within me and heal it with his own body. Even though I wanted to say no, by then, I felt an undeniable oppression, and was hopelessly vulnerable. There were several such rituals, some with candles, others not. It was always unspeakably vile, lying face down beneath him, and I felt disgusting and terribly shameful, even though I believed it was necessary.

He also managed to convince someone very close to me that she was demon possessed. It was horrific watching him on top of her. I vividly remember the revulsion on her face. Looking up at me, she shed no tears, spoke no words, and uttered not one cry. The pain in my heart was staggering as her soul appeared to slip away from her eyes, while the sickening, pungent air hung densely amid her body and his labored breathing. I wanted desperately to run out of the room. Instead, I remained and held her hand, trying to be of some comfort, while plunging deeper into my own quicksand of overwhelming fear and self-loathing.

Not too long after this, I returned to live with my dad and stepmom. Not much more than six months had passed, but I was a different person. They never really understood the magnitude of my suffering, nor did they know what had happened. Secrecy, again. Totally withdrawn into the darkest depths of insecurity, fear, and all-consuming hatred, I pretended to be as normal as possible while I finished my high school education.

Leaving home at eighteen, it wasn't long before I ended up on the streets of Vancouver with the wrong kind of friend and her beguiling promises. For a while, we survived on government food stamps, and slept in cockroach-infested beds at a scroungy hotel in China Town. I remember stealing a can of cleaning agent to scour the hotel's disgusting community bathtub.

My friend convinced me to panhandle, coming up with elaborate stories for us to swindle unsuspecting tourists, and then she slowly indoctrinated me into prostitution. By age nineteen, I was working the streets alone. In my tarnished eyes, I was already evil anyway.

It took me four years to abandon street life and the brutal drugs that kept me mollified therein. It was an insanely rough life, often on the run from police, and I spent numerous nights in jail being mocked and harassed. Truth be told, it was only by the underlying guidance of infinite intelligence that I avoided certain death during frequent close calls with se- verely corrupt street people, shady law enforcement, and the "clientele" in cars or otherwise.

Ultimately, I gained freedom from the streets with my life intact.

Since that time, I have climbed a million mountains of anger and rage, leaving a trail of destructive consequence. My life was permeated with dark secrets, self-abuse, and absolute dysfunction as I stumbled along, reacting to the world around me. I was filled with extreme hatred, for myself and ev- erybody else, but as always, I pretended to be normal.

Then, suddenly one day, I fainted, collapsing onto the cement floor at a basement party. I awoke to an overwhelming spiritual proclamation in my mind. Something powerful was compelling me to get my act together, and at thirty years old, my heart was profoundly shaken with an urgency to find "my calling" on this planet.

I immediately started searching for the source of that spiritual mes- sage, and thus embarked on a sincere journey of forgiveness, first for my- self, and then for all other people.

Studying various religions, I embraced their beliefs and endured well-meaning exorcisms, and eventually developed an understanding of universal spirituality. Studying the mind, I absorbed numerous behavior- al courses, sought professional counseling, and spent countless hours in group sessions with hundreds of wounded people.

By observing and interpreting human nature, I learned that my own behavior was normal, considering. Mercifully, employers of incredible patience somehow understood not to abandon me, and sincere, angelic friends came forth, constantly holding me up by providing unconditional love.

Throughout the healing process, my piano and poetry struggled to re- emerge. Yet it wasn't until 1998, when my grandma passed, that I began writing piano music again, picking up from my lonely child-self at the lake- side home. Poetry transpired into lyrics, and my music slowly became a venue of forgiveness and atonement.

Recently, I was honored to write a powerful message about people standing together to make our world a better place, and in a magical full circle, my lonely childhood composition joined forces with a lyrical declaration of love and acceptance.

A few years ago, at fifty-five years wise, I went to a psychologist to find out my state of mind. When posed with my biggest question, she assured me that, "Were you indeed crazy, you certainly would not be asking about it." We had a great laugh, and over several months, she eventually convinced me to believe that I had indeed found wholeness and strength.

Pondering the monstrous effects of sexual and mental abuse on a developing child, I must acknowledge a misguided older cousin who felt motivated to masturbate before my childhood eyes. What twisted exposure had established such misplaced sexual entanglement in his teenage mind, eventually manipulating him to commit suicide as a young adult? How many others are dead in their sorrows?

Ultimately, my healing transpires through continual emphasis on love and forgiveness. As a young teenager, I launched a quest seeking peace in the outermost regions of our universe, but what I finally discovered is that peace comes with knowing the pure love of our divine source, of which I am a part. For years, I chose to remain entrapped within a vicious repeating cycle of fear and dysfunctional emotion. Understanding that I am spiritual energy navigating life as a human being has given me the courage to rise out of my prison created by circumstance and accumulated influences. I am humbled and grateful, realizing that source energy was always there, steadily guiding me toward a better way of thinking.

Now, with purposeful feeling and a determined focus, I allow purifying waves of infinite love to cascade gracefully through my beautiful heart. My calling in life is to shine this love into the darkness of secrecy and suffering, to bring awareness, hope, and healing. I'm not alone in this endeavor, for the divine presence of our spiritual source is with me always, and I live in gratitude knowing that this homeland of spirit is the reason that I'm alive and surely rising.

Shining Through Double Grief
by Elizabeth Gagnon

At the age of four, I was raped by my uncle, and it forever changed my life. Then at the age of fourteen, I became pregnant with his child, after many years of his sexual abuse. My daughter was stillborn at five-and-a-half months old; she weighed one pound, twelve ounces. My first grief as a mother, losing her this way, has also forever impacted my life. Since I was a child myself at the time, I didn't understand why it happened or what stillborn was.

Not hearing my daughter cry and not being able to hold her traumatized me for years, and still affects me to this day. If I could go back to that day, the one thing I would do is hold her. Back then, when a child was stillborn, you had three options: bury or cremate, donate to science, or toss them out as it was not considered a living birth. So, you can imagine the pain I felt being given these options at age fourteen.

At the time, I was living with my alcoholic father and stepmom. My father stated that he refused to waste his money to bury a bastard child, as he called her. This statement would have a lasting impact on our relationship for years to come, even up to the day he passed away. He told me, "I signed your baby off to science. If you want to see her, go to Science North in Sudbury. She's in a tube there."

Even to this day, I often wonder if that was even true. I was given permission to name my daughter, then was told to never speak of her again or I would be sent away. Whenever I did something my parents wanted to conceal from everyone in the family, they would send me off to psychiatric hospitals. Often stating I was *crazy* or a *nut* and that the nuthouse was waiting for me again. Many years of mental and emotional abuse was handed down from both of them.

So, I kept my daughter Ashley a *secret* for many years. But every year, in secret, I would celebrate in my own way with a cup of tea and a candle on December 13.

The grief of her passing is an everyday struggle. I often wonder if we would have been close, if she would be married or have kids. I believe in my heart that she is with me every day pushing me to stay strong and continue on. I know that my baby girl who laid so still on that day has given me the strength to fight, stand tall, never, ever give up on myself, and be the mom I am today. Yes, that little girl gave me all of that. She gave me a *light to shine* through my grief. As one of my favorite songs as a child was "This Little Light of Mine" said, "I'm gonna let it shine." I believe my little girl knew. Call it a message from an angel.

In 2006, after leaving an abusive and narcissistic husband of sixteen years, I had a nervous breakdown from past emotional and mental stress and overworking and pushing myself beyond my limits. My family refused to help and told me to figure it out on my own. So, I did what I could and made the hardest choice of my life. My "family" told me that it would be in the best interest for my children if I signed them into the foster care system, so with a lot of pressure, I was forced to sign my children away. Even though I had handpicked foster homes for them with the understanding that when I was well again I could get them back, it was the hardest thing I had ever done.

Even so, losing them in this way was my second enormous grief as a mother. After placing my children in care, I fell into a very deep depression. I didn't care if I lived or died. I just wanted everything to be numb so I wouldn't cry or feel anymore.

I fought everyday with my thoughts and feelings—the what-ifs, should haves, could haves, and would haves. I grieved for bedtime stories, homework assignments, cooking, cleaning, nagging, and, most of all, the growing together and the connection between a mother and her children. I grieved hard for my living children, which is hard for others to understand. Many times, I was told they were happy and better off, that I should be grateful that they were alive, and how I should just go on with my life as they were in good homes. What a slap in the face.

I know what it is like to lose a baby at birth, and I know what it feels like to lose your living children through no fault of your own. People just don't get it unless they live it. How dare they? How dare they tell me how to feel and live?

It was arranged that, for the first eight years, I had four hour visits every two weeks with my children. I also had special occasions when the foster parents allowed me there and had phone call access and letters.

But eventually, when calling to speak to my children, I was often told by the foster parents that they were busy, they were out, or to call back. The visits became fewer and fewer as the children were told, *"You don't need to do the visit if you don't want to."* What started as every two weeks became maybe once a month or every other month or a couple times a year. The connection between my children and I was broken. I no longer felt like a mom to my children, which caused me grief in many ways.

I was often asked to wait for a visit or reschedule it for another time, which, in turn, never happened. My children knew me as Mom by name but didn't look at me as a mother anymore. They became cold, distant, and were often very rude toward me and were never told it was wrong to behave that way by their so-called peers. I would often have to bring food, games, and arts supplies to the Children's Aid Services (CAS) building in order to have a visit with my children. Even during stormy weather, which I had to walk in, I went, refusing to miss any possible time with my kids.

With no support from the CAS, if I was unable to make it to their scheduled visitation appointment, I was told, "Oh well, that is your loss. You either find a way or you won't have your visits." I was numb, how could this be happening?

Many of my visits with my children were made at ridiculous hours by their foster parents; for example, visits at 5:30 a.m. for horseback riding lessons for my oldest, or their preplanned schedules that I would have to do with my children. Most of these preplanned visits did not allow me any personal time with my children. Then CAS told me that I had to take parenting classes if I still wanted my visits, which I did, of course, because I knew if I didn't, I would never see my children again.

I was treated like an unfit mom. I was made to look like I had parenting issues because I suffer from complex post-traumatic stress disorder, depression, conversion disorder, borderline personality disorder, and an eating disorder. Then things got even worse. I was informed that I needed to have supervised visits if I still wanted to see my children. *What was going on?*

I found out that CAS and the foster parents had stated in their reports that the children would become upset if I was alone with them. I was being treated like a criminal, which I didn't understand, as I was the one who turned to them for help in the first place. So why was I being treated this way? I felt betrayed and misunderstood by CAS and the foster parents. *How did this happen?*

So supervised visits it was, as I had nothing to hide. Ironically, the supervisor that attended my visits could not understand why she was there. The children laughed, had fun, and often would say, "Mommy, you remember when you did that for us?" Like baking and cooking together or making art together, etc. The supervisor was more concerned with how the children acted when it was time to go back to foster homes. They would often hide in the closets or under the beds and scream, "No, Mommy, we want to stay with you!"

Talk about gut-wrenching pain. "If only I could," I would say to myself. My eyes would fill up with tears, and I would try to stay strong as I buckled them into the cars and gave them hugs goodbye, telling them, "I will see you soon." I would have lots of tears after they would leave, and I would cry for days and blame myself, saying things like, "Yeah, you're an awful mom," or "They're your children, what is wrong with you?"

So, I took it upon myself to show my kids that no matter what happens in life, I will always be here for them whenever they need me. I can't change the past, but I sure as hell can change the future, so I am taking the grief I live with and choosing to shine on.

With time, my kids are slowly coming back to me, seeing that all I have ever wanted was for them to be happy. I am stepping up and being the mom they need. I am accepting and giving them space when needed and giving a helping hand when I can, the best I can, with words of encouragement and support to continue on, even on their hard days, with lots of mommy hugs and tea.

Over the years, I have made a good, healthy support system with friends and services. I took tools from each of them that I incorporated into my life that I call my toolbox. I learned to stand and own who I am.

Not what others expect or want from me, that is for sure. I have found strength, courage, and awareness to own my choices, which, in turn, has gotten me through my double grief. Grief has taught me that I have unconditional love for my children and that they are always going to be a part of me and no one can take that away from me. For those reasons alone, I will shine on and be the role model my children need. I will own my story and be proud of it because it made me who I am today.

Sometimes, the hard storms in life have brought me to my lighthouse to shine on alone. I'm not quite sure what keeps me moving forward. Some days, maybe self-determination, inner strength or willpower to never give up and be defeated by any hardships in life. Losing a child as a child, losing my children after many hard years of abuse and no family support, growing up alone and on the sidelines due to childhood abuse. All my life, I searched for help, and I realized that the only one saving me, was me. That little light of mine, I made it shine.

I have found that anything is fixable as long as you put the work into it. The broken can become mended and sealed in a new light (new life). I hope that if you have ever had to place your children in someone else's care in order to keep them safe or give them what they deserve, you know you're not alone. I understand. Together, we all need to speak out and be the change for others who ask for help.

For those parents who lost a child to stillbirth or miscarriage, I understand. We need to celebrate our babies and know that they matter as well. We need to speak out to bring awareness. Yes, I had a child, but the angels took her home. Support and understanding is needed. Yes, I grieve the living as well. I will speak out. *Yes*, life is hard, but I am harder.

Today, I have a relationship with my children, and my children are proud of me and say it quite often. We have all come a long way through open communication, respecting each other's spaces, supporting one another, and accepting that things were hard once, but it is no longer holding any of us back. I honor and celebrate my beautiful daughter who passed, who chose me to be her mom knowing that she would forever live with me and through me. Her legacy will never be forgotten, and she will forever be in my heart.

Today I speak out on hard subjects that no one wants to hear. I stand and speak my truth. I give my children courage to know that they can make it too. I set an example through actions and not just with words. My voice may still shake but my story will be told, and I will shine through my double grief in a new light—through unconditional love for my children.

By sharing my story of grief, I hope I give you some understanding, courage, and a voice for you to share your own. I hope to help build a connection for those who suffer in silence and to help them shine brighter. Just like a diamond, we all sparkle and shine in our own way through grief. I'm shining on through sharing.

I Hope You Dance
by Patricia Dalgleish

As a little girl, I remember walking through the fields, releasing the sweet smell of clover. It brings back refreshing memories. My dog, Shadow, staying close and listening to my stories. She always listened and was happy to be by my side.

I am the youngest of nine children who grew up on a farm in northern Alberta. During my younger years, I remember playing outside with the animals, playing card games, and dancing until dawn. Beautiful memories.

A feeling of comfort would settle me as my first-grade teacher watched over me, sitting me closest to her. She made me feel that I mattered.

Grade two, however, was different. I recall feeling judged, not accepted. My teacher was a dentist's wife and being clean was important to her. I remember routine inspections, feeling insecure about showing my hands. Would I pass? Were my fingernails clean? Naturally, mine were not. I spent so much time outside, and we only bathed once a week. Fear of speaking to her made me freeze. Questions to her, in my reality, were not an option. A puddle formed under my desk as my face turned red. This was the day I lost part of me, my worthiness.

The rest of my elementary years are somewhat of a blur. I remember by grade six, I would seek new friends each week. Sadly, those kids were the ones the "popular" girls would pick on. I somehow preferred to be with the underdogs. I didn't feel good enough to belong. Adding to the unworthiness, more than one person challenged me sexually. They preyed on my lack of confidence.

On the farm, I spent hours with the animals; my dog, Shadow, calves, kittens. We had grand times getting the turkeys to chase us around and around the granaries, then jump in and watch the turkey go wild with his squawking like he was going to lose his marbles. Belly giggling as the turkey lost control. We chased cows to change pastures. I can recall running in the bush, fighting off mosquitos by swishing branches through the air, feeling alive as I ran in nature, connecting to the earth. I also loved to hover in the shadows and scare my sister, Pauline. She seemed to fall for it every time, which brought me great satisfaction. Every now and then, I hide and scare my husband when he least expects it. It satisfies a mischievous pleasure from my younger years. I also recall Mom floating on the dance floor. I could feel and see her pure joy.

My parents were unable to express themselves, yet I could feel the energy of their love. Expressing their feelings was not a part of their skills. My dad's nickname for me was Little Girl. My mom's expression of love was baking. We would step into the house after school on a cold winter day, thrilled at the smell of Mom's cinnamon buns lingering in the air. Mom had a way of listening to children and usually referred to them as "pumpkin" or "sweet pea." Mom also carried sadness—her mom passed away during childbirth. At thirteen, she became a mom to her two-year-old brother. She lost her childhood to become a lifetime nurturer to those around her.

Despite the love and nurturing I felt from my parents, and even though in junior high school, I finally had friends, the little voice from my younger years whispered in my ears that I was not good enough.

Dancing carried on in my teenage life, giving me a strong feeling of belonging. As a young woman of twenty-five, my hometown friends and I loved dancing and hanging out at country bars in the city. Dancing gave me a deep sense of my childhood playfulness. I had given up on ever meeting someone and instead, focused on fun. I met Lorne, my husband, when I had a few too many whiskies in the bar; he noticed me because I was being loud.

Our first date was special, the revolving restaurant and stepping into a reality that I said I would never do—be with a man who was divorced and also had three kids.

We just clicked. He was raised on a farm, we understood each other. We had such a similar childhood. I became a part of a family—Shaun, Ashley, and Aline were now my stepchildren. My parents and family opened their arms to my step kids.

In May 1993, Lorne and I were married by the Universal Church of Love on St. Thomas Island.

After that, my insecurities rose to the surface. Could I accept myself as good enough to be loved? Could he love me enough as his second wife, not his first choice? He was patient with me. My self-critic would run thoughts: How could I possibly be good enough to have his full love when he'd already given it away?

During the first months of our marriage, I had the bitter experience of watching my mom go through cancer. I can remember sitting next to Mom, the words bluntly spoken by the doctor:

"You have two weeks to live."

These words were harsh to the ears.

In August 1993, my mom passed away in our family home on the farm with all of us kids near. There is an ache within my heart because I lost Mom when I was twenty-seven, yet I am also grateful for my last conversation with her.

She was sitting up on the pull-out bed in the middle of the living room. We discussed my brother, Dennis; she was worried that he would be alone. We also talked about the chickens—collecting eggs was a fear-facing adventure. Opening the door, container in hand, ready to collect the eggs while keeping a keen eye out for the roosters, and ready to run without cracking any eggs. It is the little things that carry strong, fond, and silly memories. The last thing I said to her was that when I have a baby girl, I will name her "Josie" after her.

She said, "That would be nice."

We hugged, and she passed away a day later early in the morning.

Our son, Drew, was born in 1996. Even when he was a toddler, he had a sense of being secure with himself. Over the years, he taught me that you can be comfortable within, while not being part of the "popular" group. My baby girl was born in 1998, and yes, her name is Josie. In the beginning, when I said her name, it would bring tears to my eyes or even a lump in my throat with memories flooding in from my last conversation with Mom.

Now, Josie is twenty, and she owns her name. She's taught me that taking things personally is a waste of time and forgiving can be easy.

In November 2009, we were on a holiday with our two youngest. In the middle of the night, it was almost like someone was nudging me. At 2:00 a.m., I woke up with a tingling feeling in my breast; as I scratched at it, I discovered a lump, a pea sized bead. My eyes wide open with thoughts, staring at the ceiling, as the fears of cancer wouldn't allow sleep.

Countless times, I had to get naked and show my body to many people. The burnt smell of flesh and smoke rising as a sample of your body is taken is an unpleasant memory. The breast cancer diagnoses came in January 2010; I was forty-four. Once I heard the doctor say cancer, I really was numb and in a fog. And so my journey began. The first step was a double mastectomy with reconstruction surgery. It was a thirteen-hour surgery followed by months of recovery. During healing, a big accomplishment was walking from the bedroom to the chair in the living room, sitting for fifteen minutes, then falling asleep again. My husband remembers that the light in my eyes was dim, while my stepdaughter, Aline, thought I was stoned. Either way, I was not aware.

Agony swept over my heart when facing the difficult task of sharing with my kids the tough news: "Your mom has cancer." Josie was twelve at the time. During my recovery, there were times when she had to shower me. I carried guilt about that for a while, but now I have concluded that it is part of her journey. Our son, Drew, was fourteen at the time, and this news gave him the reality that he could lose his mom. Aline, my stepdaughter, a young adult and a new mom, stopped by every other day to clean and help me. She made me feel loved and supported as my husband continued the routine of work. Shaun, as a young man expecting his first child, stopped in when he could. Ashley would come and just hang out and clean. All three of my stepchildren, I am so grateful for, as they were supportive to me when I felt like life had kicked me in the boobs.

My dear husband, Lorne. It's so hard to watch a loved one suffer and go through trauma; sometimes it hurts more than the person who is walking the path. I appreciate his love. Cancer has softened his soul.

As time passed, I physically recovered, but emotionally, the fear of getting cancer consumed my thoughts. On a whim, when I was able to drive again. I chose to attend a body-mind expo, and it changed my life.

There, I met my mentor, Carole, who gave me the gift of a self-acceptance journey through her course, Psychosomatic Therapy Process. It was a spiritual path to self-love. Since childhood, I had been carrying feelings of not being enough, giving to others and not to myself. When we as humans are not at ease with ourselves, it leaves room for dis-ease to form. Through the work, I found peace and began the path to let go of self-judgement. Old patterns can creep up from time to time. I had a fear that I would be like my mom and get cancer a second time. The loop of my thoughts had to be altered.

Thoughts, words, and fears can bite us in the ass. I was diagnosed a second time with a reoccurrence of cancer January 2013. I ended up making the decision to remove the masterpiece the plastic surgeon made for me—I had a third mastectomy. It plain and simply sucks to have only one breast. My body suffered from mild cording, which is a rope-like structure that sometimes develops from a full mastectomy. It caused a persistent ache, but physio and essential oils helped. I am grateful lifelike prosthetics are available now, but it still sucks.

As I lay on the radiation table understanding full well that I was being poisoned for my greater good, I concentrated on moving my feet. Moving my feet is a tool so I am in my body rather than playing the fears in my mind.

Even while I was being treated, I was able to continue with the psychosomatic therapy process. I understand that the words I choose affect my reality. I made peace with the possibility that I may die soon. When walking through the challenges of cancer, I had to choose to live. I wanted to be here to raise our kids, and I wanted to be here for their weddings and their kids.

In the process of this work, fighting was not what I wanted to do. It seems to me that when we focus on fighting against something, it seems to give it more attention. Instead, I decided to walk the path to healing, to recovery, and emotional freedom to feel the connection to Mother Earth and ease within—just as I did on our farm as a child. It is ongoing work, in my human experience.

My conclusion is that my mother's path is not my path. Because she died from the disease does not mean I have to. Psychosomatic therapy process taught me that cellular memory is passed on from generation to generation. It was important to deal with my baggage, so our children can focus on their own lessons in life. I feel like I let go of some of the sadness my mom carried, and now I am focused on learning and growing each day to be a stronger, more vibrant human being that plays a role in the lives of others.

Each memory, I consider to be part of my past life. I now carry courage and strength because of cancer. I am no longer so fearful. I speak in front of crowds, express myself, share my stories, and take chances. And I still dance.

Dancing has been an immense part of my life—in my childhood, as a teenager and young adult having a blast dancing with friends, and as an ongoing deep connection with my husband. Dancing reminds me that living life with fun, playfulness, and enjoyment, is what makes me thrive. I choose to dance rather than sit on the sidelines of my own life. The refrain of Lee Ann Womack's song, "I Hope You Dance" matches it perfectly for me: "When you get the choice to sit it out or dance...I hope you dance."

The Dream of Answers
by Carol Black

My healing began in my mid-twenties, after a wildly graphic dream filled with both familiarity and chaos. I realized then that I could start on my road to forgiveness and let go of the shame associated with the traumatic events in my past. The dream provided answers, if I was open and willing to accept them.

I had always been spiritually curious and was constantly searching for answers that would help me understand why I had been sent on a life path that included abandonment, abuse, and rape. Since my mid-teens, I had devoured book after book, tried meditation, crystals, affirmations, readings, and having conversations with other seekers; but I never really told anyone my secrets and why I felt confused and ashamed. I remember I could not even say the words—incest, abuse, or rape.

During my journey, I found the Ascendant Bookstore in my hometown of Edmonton. It was filled with wonderful treasures and so many avenues to learn and research. One particular medium they offered was cassette tapes you could listen to (on a Walkman, yes, I'm from that generation) before falling asleep at night and set the intention to be shown answers in your dreams. What a wonderful idea!

I had been listening to a "past life regression" tape nightly for about two weeks when a powerful vision was shown to me through a bizarre dream. There I was, living in medieval times in a part of a castle—not the Buckingham Palace type of castle, but more like part of a tall, gray stone building that basically provided shelter. In this castle, I lived with many other family members and with my husband. I did not see any children of my own, so I guess that was not part of the message I needed to receive. In the dream, my husband was an old, short, obese man who was mean and aggressive to everyone. He would constantly abuse me in all ways.

On this particular night, there was some sort of celebration, and there were many people at the long, wooden table eating and drinking; it was loud and messy. I recall small animals like chickens, cats, and such—probably rats, too, but I can't think about that—scurrying about in the straw spread out in the corner of the main room. Several candles burned and melted over the old, wooden table holding platters of meat, kettles of vegetables, and many metallic jugs of wine.

The loud night became the early morning, and I made my way up the cold, stone, round stairway to our room. My husband soon stumbled up and was standing over me. I remember clearly how useless my struggle was to try and stop him from further injuring my body and pushing himself inside me. I found him vile and was totally revolted by his presence. Unfazed, he pressed a piece of clothing over my face and continued to rape me. I felt totally powerless.

When I awoke from this dream, I was sobbing and gasping for air, but I knew I had just witnessed something significant. My past-life dream had shown me that the abusive husband from my dream was now my adoptive father in my present reality. His behavior during that medieval time was not according to his proposed life plan, and therefore, he needed to try and live a better life this time, which included making amends to me. This time, instead of being vulgar and abusive, he was showing me overly inappropriate love and unwanted physical touching. On the other side of the coin, he was a caring family man who never lost his temper, rarely drank alcohol, laughed lots, and was thoughtful and kind. His warm personality is also what made it so difficult for other family members to ever believe, to this day, that he had ever done anything sexually inappropriate to me. At the time, this made me question if it was really unacceptable or if I was exaggerating the situation. Was it really my fault?

My epiphany after the big dream was that everything that happens to me is not always exclusively about me. I can learn to forgive, let it go, and move on, and I can learn to let go of the shame that is not mine to carry. It was not my responsibility to help my dad figure out his life path, but if I could forgive him, I could let go of the burden I had been carrying.

If I truly wanted to help myself, I had a good deal of situations to examine and reflect on. At thirteen, and in the midst of the regular abuse from my dad, I was summer babysitting for my oldest brother's two kids. It was a nice sunny day and my nephew was playing outside with his friends. I was sitting with my niece on the sofa when I heard heavy feet quickly pounding up the stairs. Suddenly, there was a strange man in the middle of the hallway asking me, "Where's Joe?" I did not know Joe and quickly realized that this guy had other intentions.

He walked right past me, scanned the rest of the apartment, and then shoved me toward the bedroom doorway. Thankfully, my little niece was too young and oblivious and continued to play on the sofa with her doll, not paying any mind to this new person.

He forced me into the master bedroom, pushed me against the locked door, and held a knife to my throat while ordering me to remove my clothes. I had no idea I could experience such a feeling of terror and fear. I could smell alcohol and stale cigarette smoke from his breath as he shoved me on the bed, held a pillow over my face, and began undoing his pants. After he pried open my legs and uttered more threats, I felt something trying to break my insides apart. I did my best to keep my privates tight and impenetrable. He finally gave up trying to shove his penis inside me and started to force his way through with his fingers. Again, he held the knife blade against my throat and made more threats; he pressed the pillow harder over my face as he became more frustrated.

I really have no idea how long this lasted, probably not more than ten minutes, when he finally gave up trying, and I heard him swear and mumble in anger as he pulled his pants up. His parting warning to me was not to move or scream until he was gone or he would hurt the little girl. I lay there naked and terrified with the pillow still over my face until a few minutes after I heard his footsteps go down the stairway. I tried to scream, but there was no sound; fear literally took all control of my voice.

I managed to grab my little niece and run down the front street half-dressed and shoeless into a nearby business where the kind staff helped me. They called the police and my parents who all arrived shortly after, and we returned to search the apartment and look for my nephew. I was a shy, naïve girl, and I remember feeling extremely uncomfortable and so stupid with the uniformed policemen and the questions they were asking me. I was mortified, scared, and confused.

The rape was never discussed with me again by my family, which led me to question if they felt this attack was not "important." Or did they just simply not know how to help me? The police never did find the offender, as far as I know.

I guess this incident also made me decide that the strange love expressed by my dad was more acceptable than the sexual violation from an unknown stranger. I knew my dad was coming from a place of love, and this man was coming from a place of anger and hatred. This was all so confusing.

After this ordeal, I don't recall having much of a normal adolescence when I didn't feel afraid to be alone. I quit school in grade ten, got a job at a local pizza restaurant, and met a stable young man, three years older than me, at work. We started dating when I was fifteen, and we were engaged by the time I was seventeen; we were in love! He was a good man and exactly what I needed at that point in my life to make the transition—to move out of the house and away from the alone times with my dad into a proper loving relationship.

Then came a rude awakening, a few months before my wedding day. My brother, Dennis, was killed in a car accident at nineteen years old. I felt such an overwhelming heartbreak and sense of loss; a major part of my soul was gone. He and I had been abandoned by our birth mother and thankfully adopted together before we were both three years old. I couldn't understand why I personally had to deal with so many emotionally painful situations.

Fortunately, now I take great comfort in knowing that the bond will not be broken with our loved ones who have passed over to the other side. I can still feel my brother's presence with me forty years later. A silver lining with his passing is that I have become closer than ever to my next oldest brother, Al. I am very grateful every day for having him in my life.

I helplessly carried the powerful fear of being alone into the first few years of my new marriage. My husband was now a manager at the pizza place where we met and was often not home until three or four in the morning on weekend nights. I remember being so terrified to be alone in our apartment that I would put knives in the front door frame to keep it from opening. Then, I would curl up and hide in the bottom of the linen closet with another butcher knife until I knew he was on his way home. I am fairly sure he did not know the extreme fear I carried, and I didn't tell him about it or about my dad's abuse for many years. He became the father of my two wonderful children, and he and his family were a big influence in my young life. I was finally able to gain some confidence in myself by my mid-twenties, and I felt I needed to find my own answers, even if that meant being alone. That's when the marriage ended, and I found my way to the Ascendant Bookstore and had the dream that began my journey of healing.

Now over forty years later, I am still quite guarded and definitely over fearful of certain situations, but I am able to live comfortably alone and not be afraid. I can also talk about and share my experiences of the abuse and assault with my close friends, many of whom have been through similar experiences, some much worse than me. We are able to share and try to help each other with understanding and support, living with the realization that sexual abuse of some sort has happened to so many young girls, far more than we ever want to believe.

After my past-life dream, I know that if I am able to forgive the people who came into my life, such as my dad and the man who raped me, for their ignorance, bad judgment, and the pain they caused me, I can let my anger go. I understand that forgiveness is a very personal decision and can be an extremely difficult choice to make; in my case, it has certainly been the most healing. I can close that chapter and not carry any hate in my heart. A heart not filled with anger and hate leaves more space for love and understanding.

The Strength to Choose Me
by Bonnie Nicole

B reaking a cycle is one of the hardest things I have ever done in my life, and I've had a few that I've had to break in my lifetime. Being caught in a cycle that is ingrained from childhood is never an easy one to stop. I can only explain it like being on a hamster wheel that is uncontrollably spinning and won't slow down; the only way to get off of it is to take your opportunity and jump eyes wide open, and while you may not land on your feet, you wipe yourself off and stand tall, ready to start a new way of doing things. I have been on and off this wheel my entire life, but I finally burned the wheel down two years ago.

From a young age, I have been subjected to violence. My stepfather and mother were caught in their cycle of addictions, and I got to see first-hand what this did. My most prominent memories of their drinking include my mom covered in blood and cuts on her face and shoulder from a beer bottle and the time my stepfather poured hot sauce all over our beautiful, white Husky; these memories still haunt me today. I was a scared little girl wondering why my mom still drank when this was always the outcome. I not only learned that violence was normal but also that running away was a simple task when no one was paying attention to me. I would go to my grandma's for peace and love. I was lucky that we all lived on the same property. My parents and I lived in a small house on one side of the tennis court, and my grandma's "big house" was on the other.

I also experienced sexual abuse at a young age, which taught me how little I was worth. To this day, I do not know when the molestation began, but it continued until I was nine, and after that, the inappropriate behaviour continued. There were also times when I was the brunt of physical violence and actually yearned for it. As a child, any attention was good because it was better than nothing, as this was my normal. I literally grew up thinking I deserved anything that was thrown my way; a sad way of thinking for such a young lady with dreams to be seen and heard. Essentially, I had given up on life early on and thought I was being punished for being such a bad girl. Why else would I have been subjected to such terrible things? I believed my purpose in life was to allow others to hurt me.

I grew up to be a codependent person, so I always focused on my partners' lives and not my own. I had low self-esteem, and leaving a relationship was terribly hard for me to do. By age twenty-four, I was leaving my second codependent relationship, but this time, I was a single mom to a two and one year old. At twenty-six, I met a man who swept me right off my feet. I didn't even realize the cycle I was entering until it was too late. I was trying to start a fresh life with my kids and get out of the party scene, but I fell so hard for this man and his good looks, I didn't pay attention to any of the red flags that were constantly arising. So much destruction happened because of this relationship; losing custody of my two children and the loss of my home. I felt alone and abandoned; with nowhere to bring my kids to live, I also felt defeated. I stayed with this man, thinking he would have my back through these hard times.

The first three years were the hardest. I tried my best to visit my kids often, but I was so addicted to having this man love me that I put him before anyone else.

The first beating came as a surprise. I was addicted to Percocet and OxyContin within the first six months of this relationship, and while selling drugs to keep up the habit, I had fallen asleep during the day. I awoke to my boyfriend standing above me yelling at me for not answering the phone. My boyfriend was a solid three hundred pounds and over six feet tall, and when he said I was getting a beating, I cowered and took it. By the end of it, my face was unrecognizably puffy and black and blue all over. I looked like I had been in a car accident. Everyone knew what happened to me on the reserve, but not one person stood up and said it was wrong.

I felt alone and empty. I had no feelings other than self-pity because I truly believed I was disposable as a human. My boyfriend would look at my bruised face and say how sorry he was and how much he loved me, so I stayed and believed him.

The next time, he only hit me once, but it was a good one. When he saw blood all over his hand, he thought my face split his hand, but it was actually my brow bone that cut his hand and my face was pouring blood everywhere. His mom drove me to the hospital because I "slipped in the shower." I had family court that day as I was actively trying to regain custody of my children, but I did not make it, and once again, I looked like the mother full of excuses.

The punches were the easiest to deal with. I loved being hit; it's hard to explain, but I craved it. Heck, sometimes I would provoke it, and I would feel whole once I was put into line. The emotional abuse was a reminder of how I thought people portrayed me: ugly, fat, lazy, and on track to end up just like my mother. Every time I was spat on or put down, it chiseled a piece of my soul away, and eventually, I came to terms with my fate. This was my life, and I had better just get used to it.

I got pregnant twice and both times I was ordered to have an abortion, as my boyfriend sure as heck didn't want to have kids with me. I never questioned it, and never voiced my opinion out of fear. I wanted those babies, but he did not want me having his children. I knew better, and I would go with my head down and shamefully do what I was told. Then when I would get home, tired and emotionally drained, I was considered a lazy, worthless person for not having a clean house for him to come home to. He would call me a dirty pig and tell me to go look at myself in the mirror to see how ugly I was, and how I was going to look like my mother, drugged and used up.

He said I would never do any better than him, so I continued to stay because I was lucky someone loved me. Even when he had his buddy stay with us from Edmonton, he would order me to stay in the bedroom while they watched movies because there was no extra seat on the couch for me. I started to feel very isolated and wanted my old life back, but it seemed so unattainable to me at the time.

Then I got pregnant, but this time I had hit my breaking point. My kids had been out of my care for over two years, and in my eyes, I was keeping the baby to pay for the years I lost with my kids. My way of thinking was skewed, and my idea of love was wrong, but I had given away years to this man and it was time to do the right thing. I did not tell my boyfriend I was pregnant until I was in my second trimester, so there was no going back. I stood firm in my decision, stopped taking pills, and put 110 percent effort into getting custody of my two children back. My pregnancy was hard and lonely. I had no job, family, help, or vehicle. When my boyfriend would get mad at me, he would kick me out and I would walk to the back fields behind the reserve and lie on the cold, hard ground waiting for a call to come back and do the "walk of shame."

I always had a phone because god forbid my boyfriend did not know my whereabouts at all times, and so I could communicate with my aunt, who had custody of my children. I would be home every day and night living off whatever was left for me to eat, which was usually rice and canned salmon (I really dislike canned salmon), while my boyfriend went to parties and barbecues with his buddies and whatever girls were vying over him at the time.

When my water broke, my boyfriend was sleeping, so I woke him up saying, "It's time to go." To no surprise to me, he did not care, and so I found a ride from someone else and had the hardest labour I have ever experienced. I am forever grateful to my then sister-in-law for sticking it out with me from the minute we got to the hospital until the moment my son was born; she even cut the umbilical cord. When he finally saw the baby, the first words out of my boyfriend's mouth were, "He's not mine."

I gave birth to my son on May 3, 2010, and regained full custody of my oldest two on May 5, 2010. The drinking crept in after a few months of being alone with three kids every day. My boyfriend was out playing ball a few times a week and going to the gym daily with his new best friend. He would never bring us, offering excuses like there was no room, or he's driving someone else, or, or, or he simply was embarrassed by his girlfriend with the three kids.

I would drink vodka every night when the kids would go to bed and get drunk enough to pass out on the couch. I taught my children to be quiet and tiptoe around him because he was like the big grumpy bear. When our relationship was good, it was great, but when it was bad, it was terrible. He had stopped hitting me after our son was born, but he had no trouble spitting on me and calling me names that made me feel worthless. I literally felt like a waste of space in this world, but I had to learn to live in this world for my children so they could be together because I did not think I could do this alone. I had never even rented a place in my life, let alone rented one with three kids.

One day, after my youngest turned three, my daughter didn't come home. I got the phone call that changed my life. She wasn't coming home unless home was somewhere without my abusive boyfriend. The fighting was constant, and I realized it was not only taking a toll on me and my mental health, but also on my children. To this day, my youngest cannot stand the sound of arguing, and I firmly believe this came from all the yelling that took place throughout the pregnancy and first years of his life.

It took me six days to find a place and move in, but that wasn't the end of the cycle. My boyfriend took a hockey stick to me that week and punched one of my helpers moving me. He harassed me for months to follow, and I admittedly allowed him into my house for about a month before I finally knew we were not destined for each other. It was when even the sound of his breathing bothered me that I knew I was done. I was finally free of him and did not feel the need to take care of him over myself.

What followed was my spiral into extreme drug abuse, a court case against my ex, and me finding out how to live alone as a single mother. I honestly failed at the job, and it wasn't for another three to four years before I finally got sober for the last time in my life and realized I was a product of my upbringing and that I was very codependent. I still saw myself as an ugly, worthless waste of skin, but after being free of all relationships and being single for the first time in my life, I began to really see the damage my past relationships had done to me.

As of now, I am a single mom and stronger than ever. I am now aware of my patterns and know what to look for in a relationship. Now when I see red flags or have a gut feeling, I take action! I no longer need to be abused to feel loved because I have my children and a great group of mentors and friends who love me. Being in an abusive relationship may have made me stronger on the outside, but mentally, it tore me down to my knees.

I am grateful to be where I am today, speaking on stages and sharing my message with the world. I recently did a Facebook challenge called "The 100 Days of Confidence," and the number of women who religiously posted along with me each and every day was astounding. It is amazing to me what can be done when we link arms and support one another. We get one life, so make it count.

Breaking the Great Silence
by Rika Harris

This story goes back a long way, over thirty years, but it is still with me, and now it wants to be told.

When I got married, I knew I wanted a big family. Although our financial situation was far from ideal, I did not see any point in waiting for the "right time" to come around.

Pregnant within a year, I grew big and heavy and I glowed. I delivered a healthy baby boy, recovered quickly, and began the exciting, frightening, and demanding job of looking after my new baby. I settled into motherhood with many apprehensions and misgivings. It was not always easy, but I did trust my instincts a fair bit, and my son grew and thrived.

In time, after about a year, I felt ready to try for another baby. This time, I became pregnant almost right away. At around twelve weeks, I had some bleeding which alarmed me, but it seemed to go away again. I felt let off. However, the bleeding and heavy cramps returned, and within two days, the pregnancy was over. I was devastated and actually quite ill afterward.

We were assured by our doctor that no damage had been done, to wait a while, and try again. It was hard to accept the loss. I had always had problems with depression in the past and struggled again after the loss. The fact that I had a child to look after kept me going somehow.

About six months later, I was pregnant again. This time, I was watching my body closely and anxiously. Since things had gone wrong before, I became hyperaware of any potential signs of trouble, and I frequently checked in with my body; any twinge or little cramp made me afraid of what might be going on and that it might happen again. Still, I felt well and hopeful for a good outcome.

It was not to be. At nine weeks this time, after some bleeding and cramps, according to the ultrasound scan, the pregnancy just disappeared. This hit me hard. I could not understand why this was happening to me. I felt utterly alone. I lived in England at the time, felt like an outsider and unaccepted, and could not share my feelings of grief and loss with anyone.

I was scared to try again and was beginning to come to terms with having an only child, but then, I became pregnant again. This time, I was even more aware of my body, and particularly during the earlier "dangerous" weeks, I was totally obsessed with checking that I was not bleeding. Every little sign of pain in my reproductive area was like a sign of imminent doom. The anxiety and fear of something going wrong again was so intense it almost consumed me.

Bit by bit, the weeks passed. After the twelve-week ultrasound scan was clear, I started to relax and enjoy the pregnancy.

It turned out that the baby stayed transverse, but I was told this could still change. I became big and round, and the baby was active. I had a routine checkup with my doctor at thirty-four weeks. He thought the baby was small (still transverse) and requested another ultrasound scan. It was not urgent, and the appointment took two weeks to come through. I had to drive into Oxford to the university clinic and my son came with me. He was getting used to these checkups and was okay waiting the few minutes for the scan.

In those days, it was still required to change into a gown for the scan. I got called in, got on the bed, and the technician started. I couldn't make out much on the screen. She was very quiet. When I asked her about the heartbeat, she just said she was not sure and had already called the specialist in. I did feel uneasy at that but not alarmed. The specialist appeared soon after and did his check also.

I remember watching him anxiously, and then he turned to me and said, "We can detect no sign of life."

I clearly heard these words, and I could feel them in my brain. They were just floating around unable to connect anywhere. It seemed an age, and then these words landed—no sign of life meant the baby was dead!

I just went to pieces. It was too much to grasp. It could not be true. But it was. I was helped off the bed and sat on a chair. I could not take it in. The only thought that hammered in my head was the baby is dead. At thirty-six weeks, I had been so close to full term. This was not right; this could not be.

Eventually, I was able to get back to the cubicle to change back into my clothes. It was there that a line from a book I'd read popped into my head. It described a character I loved: "She had no children of her own, and she became mother to all."

I remember thinking, is that it, is that the message? Am I meant to follow that example? I knew I already had a son I loved dearly, but my heart wanted to be wide open for more.

Then and there, I surrendered. I let it be. I gave up control and moved into some kind of acceptance. My body and mind were numb with shock and loss and grief, but somehow my heart knew that I did not need to fight what happened. There was a lesson that I did not yet understand or even want, but it was there for me to accept. This did not take the loss or the pain away, but it gave me something to cling to. I had to let go of control and outcomes; I had to fall into trust even though, at that time, I had no such concept. It was simply a natural flow.

When my husband arrived, it was arranged that we should go home and come back the next day so labor could be induced. I found it cruel to be sent home as if all was normal. I could not do it. We stayed with friends instead.

As we were leaving, of course we encountered other hugely pregnant women, and I was jealous of them; their babies were still alive. It was so hard to take in what had happened. Despite my willingness to accept the situation, feelings of pain, sadness, and loss were pulsing through me and sometimes nearly drowning me.

I made it through the night, somehow. The next afternoon we went back, and I was placed in a small room with just one bed—privacy for what was to come. I was induced, and I remember it took some hours to deliver.

When she was born, she was tiny, and a nurse placed her in my arms. I did want to see her, even though I was nervous and did not know what to expect. Wrapped up in her blanket, she actually looked totally normal and beautiful. As this was way before digital cameras, the nurse offered to take some Polaroids and then left us alone for a while. My husband and I took turns cradling her and giving her cuddles and kisses. We wanted to give her all the love we had in our hearts for her. This was the only thing we could do, the only time we had.

When the nurse returned, the baby was in my arms. Well, I had previously read about people who carried a dead baby or child and how they did not want to release the body. I had thought that to be exaggerated or made up. Now I know better. It was the hardest thing to open my arms to let her go. I really just wanted to hold her forever. It was all I could give her, and to me at that moment, it was so precious and meaningful. I know I had to do it, but oh, what a heart-wrenching moment. This was it; my beautiful beloved baby was gone.

I do not remember how I got through the night. The next day, still in hospital, we saw various officials and also the undertaker. He assured us that we could see her one more time before the funeral. I was happy about that; to see her one more time seemed a great gift.

Many thoughts and emotions then beset me. One of the worst thoughts was that I was a horrible mother because I had not felt that my baby was dead. How could I not have known that? How could I not have felt it? She had apparently been dead for at least a week. I talked to one of the midwives because I had felt movement, which I had thought was the baby moving. She told me it had likely been the womb shifting the baby about. Treacherous body, misleading me like that!

And then, of course, the torturous idea that I might have done something wrong, eaten the wrong diet, done something or not done something, that maybe it could have been otherwise, that this was somehow my fault. It was not until several weeks later that I learned it had been a chromosome abnormality—chromosome 18 had tripled—and nothing could have changed the outcome. Only then did I give up on these thoughts, this kind of self-torture.

The next few days crept by. I was preparing for the undertaker to let us know when we could see our little girl one more time. I managed to get a white rose from a friend and also a bunch of white sweet peas. I was pretty well ready now to see my baby again and could think of little else. Finally, the undertaker came to see us to tell us that, in his opinion, it was not a good idea to view the baby again. My husband, never one to rock the boat, simply agreed.

I was so stunned, I think I turned to stone. I was unable to utter a single word. Inside, I was screaming, "Do I have to give this up as well?" All my planning, my wish to say goodbye and see her one last time? Inwardly, I felt again that I had to give up control, but outwardly, I was frozen. The undertaker left and my husband finally looked at me. For once, he perceived my feelings, which was not usual for him. He asked, "You wanted to see her again, didn't you?"

I just nodded. I have to give him credit; he dashed out the door and caught the undertaker still turning around his car. He told him we had changed our minds and wanted to see her anyway.

When we got to the mortuary and entered, there was this tiny Styrofoam box on a small table, about the size of a shoebox. I cannot remember anything else in the room. I was totally fixated on this tiny coffin. I was nervous again because of what the undertaker had said, but when he opened the lid, she was still beautiful.

I used all the sweet pea blossoms and placed them around her face. It looked like a garland, and I put the rose beside her. She was so pretty and peaceful, wrapped in her blanket and with the flowers around her, and I knew I would remember this picture in my head forever. I was so, so grateful that I did have the chance to do this for her after all, and it was good. It seemed little, but it was intensely meaningful for me.

After that, we needed to get back on with our lives, hard as it was to come to terms with all that had happened. I did remember the thought about being a "mother to all" and registered as a childminder. Within a few weeks, in addition to raising my own son, I was looking after someone else's little girl.

I grieved and I cried and missed my little girl terribly. My friends and family were caring and understanding, but after a while, they didn't mention it much. As if there was a kind of time limit on grieving and sadness. I think many people simply don't know what to say. So, stories like mine get added to the Great Silence.

This all happened many years ago for me, but once the idea of sharing it came to me, this story insisted on being told. It is not morbid. It is not crazy to share. It is not sick still to remember after all these years.

I think way too many women of all ages have kept such stories of grief or loss or trauma of any kind in their hearts, unable to share because who would want to listen?

I would.

For anyone who wants to tell their story, I am here willing to listen: with care and compassion, without judgment or distaste, holding space for you and your story. Maybe, like mine, your story also wants to be told.

My Awakening
by Sheree Agerskov

A s I sit down to write this chapter, I am very aware of the procrastination that has kept me from starting all morning, every morning, all month. This time is different. I realize that there hasn't been any of the usual self-doubt that fuels the procrastination. I believe in myself; I am comfortable sharing.

I feel a comfort in knowing that I have let go of shame and fear. Today, I am fully present, living and creating an amazing life. This wasn't always the case for me.

Being a self-saboteur off and on for almost fifty years was exhausting. I have indulged in very risky behaviours over the years; I have had anger issues, been very negative, and blamed others for the state of my life. I stayed in toxic relationships, ones that were going nowhere, and allowed people to treat me badly. Always searching for love and acceptance, I needed someone filling me up, taking care of me. My terrible self-image and limiting beliefs were born from early trauma.

At seven, my parents split. My mother left for another man, and when I was nine, my father took a new partner. My little brother and I were moved across the country with my father and stepmother, away from my mother. My heart ached for her; I missed my mom so much. The next few years were filled with extreme emotional, physical, and sexual abuse from my stepmom and her siblings.

She came from a large family, and I remember stories of a heavy handed and strict father. She lived and carried on what she had learned. Standing tall on our knees in the corner was a common punishment for us, and we would sometimes pass out from the discomfort. We were often there for hours, sneaking a rest when she left the room, dropping down on our calves and heels to relieve the dizziness and pain. Getting caught would send her into a violent rage that meant someone was getting a massive beating.

We were often kept home from school to spend the day in punishment. One particular time, my brother had wet the bed the night before. The wet bed sheet was draped over his face, and we knelt, in the corner.

Shaking, nauseous, and weak, I didn't dare break my corner stance. He tried to control the sobs, and his body trembled with fear. My stepmom held a large butcher knife and screamed "Piss the bed again, and I'll cut that fuckin' prick off!" He was five. I was terrified she might follow through this time, feeling so helpless as well and relieved that I was not her target at the moment.

When I was eleven, we were both sent back across the country to live with my mother. My memory is that my stepmother wanted my brother gone and my dad didn't want to split us up. For years, I felt that my father chose her over us. Today, I like to believe that he sent us away to protect us, that he was in a severely abusive relationship, and didn't have the courage to stand up to her, or to leave. Abuse can be crippling.

My mom received two very broken and traumatized children. I quickly became rebellious and angry, hiding behind a tough-as-nails attitude that didn't need anybody. I was one badass little shit, smoking cigarettes and pot and experimenting with drugs. An experience at thirteen created another layer of trauma. I never spoke of it for the next forty years. To anyone. I was ashamed.

My memory is limited, and I don't have any concept of time or many details. I only remember one man, a leader in the Satan's Choice bike gang, which ran in my area. It was a toxic underworld of organized crime. I had addictions, and he kept me high. I would completely detach from my body and do what was expected of me. I was thirteen. He was in his thirties.

A week, a month, six months? I have no idea how long this went on, or when it stopped, but at fourteen, I was committed to a psychiatric hospital because I wanted to die. My first "dark night of the soul" experience.

Shame. I really believed the biker incident was my fault. I didn't fight or say no. I was passive and cooperative. Didn't that make me a willing participant?

I spent three months and my fifteenth birthday in the hospital, and when released, I quit school and left home. Renting a room from a single mom, I sold photography packages door to door.

By sixteen, I knew I needed to make some big changes or I wasn't going to survive, and I wanted to survive. I moved back across the country to be with my father. I lived with him and my stepmother until their marriage ended that same year. She was still abusive. Very quickly, my father moved out to live with a woman and I rented his home. Over the next ten years, unconscious and unaware, I allowed life to just happen. This included many ups and downs.

At twenty-six, I fell madly in love with a man who adored me and treated me like a queen. A rescuer. Looking back on our marriage, I was often a controlling, miserable bitch. A perfectionist. And a victim. I blamed everybody for everything. If I broke a glass, it was clearly my husband's fault because he left it on the damn counter.

There were a lot of challenges in our marriage: infertility, in vitro, lost pregnancies, adoption, and raising a child severely affected by autism and other neurological disorders. She is twenty-five now and requires twenty-four seven care. My Emily is a beautiful girl, and I love her dearly. But to be honest, it was exhausting and hellish for many years.

I didn't know how to feel, and I had very limited coping skills. I just kept hiding behind my mask, pretending everything was fine. Old wounds were controlling me.

In 2009, at forty-six, I ended my twenty-year marriage. My children were sixteen and ten, and I didn't know who the hell I was. I had anger raging through me at times. I never struck my son, but during this time, I was hard on him emotionally, and I really believed I was destroying him. I am very proud of the young man he has become, in spite of all my mistakes.

My husband had stood by me through everything, and then I just walked away. He was crushed. My children were crushed. Friends could not understand, they were not supportive, and some of them were very judgmental and hurtful. I felt so much guilt, so much shame, so alone. All I could see was what a horrible, disgusting person I was.

Six months later, I was swept off my feet by a man who I would spend the next four years with. Red flags were popping up everywhere, and I ignored them. He was honest about his history with addictions and that he had been clean for a year. I was naïve. He quickly fell back into his addictions, and he became abusive and violent. He took me back to that terrified little girl who was always trying to please and keep the peace. My life was a whirlwind of chaos. He threatened my life often, once leaving his handprint bruised across my neck, taking me to the very edge of my life.

I've always had an insatiable appetite for knowledge and personal growth. Like a lonely homemaker gets lost in romance novels, I have been devouring self-help books since my early teens. During this abusive relationship, my long-time habit was a lifesaver. I read the book Codependent No More by Melody Beattie. This caused a massive shift for me. A very painful shift. Reading the list of all the personality characteristics, I recognized many of them in me, and these were not positive or pretty.

All the resistance, all the excuses, just left me. A deep and uncontrollable sadness rolled through my whole body as I realized my part in the life I was living. For three days, I cried fifty years of tears. A giant puddle—on the couch, on the carpet, on the shower floor. I cried. I was raw with overwhelming emotions that had been stuffed away for so long. I was drowning in guilt, shame, and disappointment, alone and unsupported.

I found myself in another "dark night of the soul." I was suicidal again and spent three weeks in the hospital. But what a blessing it turned out to be. I came out finally ready to accept responsibility for the life I had created and make changes. I experienced a spiritual awakening.

I spent the next year immersed in my self-care and healing. I was stronger, more self-aware, and less reactive. This man was still in my home, and his addictions were worse than ever. Then he stole $3,000 from my daughter, and it was all over. He fled across the country to avoid being arrested, and I was finally free of him.

His childhood environment was horrendous, and I can only imagine the trauma he endured. Today, I am grateful for this experience as it was the "rock bottom" that propelled me into massive growth. With him gone, I got busy treating the trauma, old and new, rewiring my brain, and recreating me.

Trauma caused a lot of physical and emotional disorders for me over the last forty plus years, and during times of crisis in my life, I have been blessed with many diagnoses: depression, chronic fatigue, fibromyalgia, ulcerative colitis, anxiety disorder, bipolar, dependent personality disorder, (during my abusive relationship) complex trauma, and of course, post-traumatic stress disorder. With only mild fibromyalgia flares today, I am emotionally, physically and spiritually balanced, healthy, and medication free.

Over the last four decades, I have explored so many paths on the way from self-loathing and self-sabotaging to radical self-love and acceptance. I have often overwhelmed myself, trying to implement too much, too quickly. I have given up, and then started again. I kept searching, learning, and incorporating what was working. Things didn't really change until I decided that I was done living a crappy life. Free of the abusive relationship, I was finally ready to take massive action.

I continued with counseling and started practicing things I had learned over the years. I yearned for an authentic, heart-centered existence. Life and love is a practice, and it's a long ass road from the head to the heart. It was time to live and practice what I had been learning.

I did Louise Hay's mirror work: looking myself in the eye and saying "I love you" over and over. Fake it till you make it.

I forced myself to get outside in the sunshine. Nature grounds me and fills me up.

I bombarded my brain any chance I got, reading and listening to self-help audiobooks and affirmations.

I became aware of my thoughts and turned them around, always looking for better feeling thoughts. Our thoughts create our emotions, and our emotions create our experiences.

I went to restorative and deep stretch yoga classes. I meditated.

I started a gratitude journal. Negativity cannot live in gratitude. Every day, I consciously searched for five new things to record that evening that I was grateful for. This forced me to be present during the day.

If I took one small step, it led to another small step, and another. Compounded, those steps have led to a daily practice that grows and changes with me. By taking action and practicing daily, I am rewiring my brain and creating new neural pathways. I am overcoming my mind, and I catch the negative thoughts when they occasionally creep in. It is a practice, and it takes time. I don't make excuses anymore. I take action.

Today, I look out the window of my office. It is pouring rain and stormy, but I need a break from writing, and Benny, my Havanese, needs a walk. As I walk along the canal in tulip-painted rubber boots, the hood on my coat keeping me dry, I am aware of the leaves dancing in the wind. The branches bending and moving in the swirling chaos of the storm. The resilience, they show. Firmly standing with deep roots, letting the wind flow through and around them without resistance.

I am the trees, I am present, right here, right now. It occurs to me how much I live this way now. I accept and let life flow. With little resistance. I see beauty everywhere, and the littlest things bring me joy. I am feeling very proud and grateful in this moment.

For the last three years, I have been building a new business. Building a new me. Finding a confidence I have never known before. Awakening to possibilities.

I know that I really do love myself because of the way I treat myself. Self-care isn't hair, nails, and pedicures. It's what creates spiritual, emotional, and physical balance. It's radical self-acceptance and self-love. Instead of sabotaging myself, as I did for so many years, I am finding purpose and passion in almost everything I do. I love my life, and I love myself.

Becoming the True Me
by Alexis Ellis

I was born a healthy, happy baby boy in Surrey, British Columbia. I was also born with cerebral palsy, which was a shock to my parents, I'm sure. With one older brother and another brother born after me, I became the middle child. I couldn't figure out why I wasn't close to my brothers, but I always felt left out. Growing up, I also had a hard time making friends, since cerebral palsy affected the way I communicated, in speaking and in writing; I still work on this constantly.

When I was about ten years old, I felt strange. I could tell I wasn't like my brothers, and I wasn't interested in the things they were doing. At my grandparents' place, I watched them spoil my girl cousin and thought, "I want to be their granddaughter, too!" Every time I'd be out and see other little girls, I wished I was them instead of me. I didn't like being a boy. At heart, I wasn't a boy. I realized I was born in the wrong body, and I wasn't happy.

Around that time, I started sneaking into my parents' room to try on my mom's clothes. She wasn't a dressy lady, but she had a few shiny, smooth things, and I loved them. I would take clothes from her and hide them in my room, and when I wore them, it felt comfortable, like I was finally dressed right.

I also thought I was weird. As I started high school, I knew it wasn't "normal" for me to look at girls and want to be like them, to wear dresses and skirts, and want to grow up to be a mother and have kids. So, as I grew up, I thought I was a pervert and kept quiet. I did my best to ignore it all.

When I was about thirty-two, I saw ads seeking drag models, so I put on makeup, wore women's clothes, and modeled a couple of times. At the time, I was living with my parents, and I didn't know what they'd think, so I didn't tell them about the modeling. But the experience felt so right that I knew something was wrong with living my life as a man.

In 2013, I started going to a transgender medical clinic, and I had to research a lot about what it meant to be a transgender woman. The doctors were great and gave me a lot of support and information. They wouldn't allow me to start on the female hormones until I knew what would happen to my mind and body, but I learned everything that I needed to know and got my new life started. I visited the clinic every few months for checkups.

In the meantime, I had been going with a guy and living with him. As I made all these changes, I decided I would be better off without him. I was scared to end it, but then he ended it first. After that, I decided that I had to tell my parents about being transgender, but I was afraid to go home. So, I told them first in an email. I told them I now had longer finger nails with polish on them. I told them I was transgender.

To my surprise, I was able to go home without any issues, and I had a long talk with my parents. They'd already noticed all the women's clothes and makeup in my room at home, they still supported me, and now they accepted me as a transgender woman. When we were done talking, my mom told me I was always supposed be her daughter and that she was happy to have a daughter now. She even said that I inspired her to try new stuff like manicures and piercings. I was so glad we had a chat.

Over the next few years, I was working two jobs and I never told my bosses or coworkers that I was transgender. Until around 2017, I was still in hiding at work. At that time, some of the staff noticed I was acting weird, and one coworker noticed I was wearing a sports bra under my undershirt and work uniform. I had been wearing women's clothes when I was off work, but only women's underwear during work hours. It was hard to live this divided life, so I decided to speak to an old manager from a past job and come out to her as a transgender woman.

She told me that I shouldn't be scared to tell the people at my current work places, as there was no way I could get into trouble or lose my job because of this. She already had a staff member who was transgender, and they were okay with it. Impressed with this news, I worked up the nerve to tell both of my bosses at my two jobs. Instead of two easy transitions, I had a rough time with the one job. I was fired, due to my employer's fears regarding her clients. Having worked for her for many years, I was so sad to lose the job, but knew it wasn't my fault. It was her beliefs that got in the way.

Losing that job was both bad and good, since it opened new doors for a new life. And, my other job fully supported me, even giving me a uniform in my right gender with my own locker room. With the support of coworkers, I still enjoy going to that job, and our customers don't mind who I am at all.

In 2016, I decided to have surgery to transition from a male to female body, although the journey didn't start until January 2017. I had to do two medical assessments to see if I was ready for the surgery, mentally and emotionally. In September 2017, I was approved for my surgery, and the date was set for March 2018. I didn't want to wait any longer, so I asked if it could happen sooner. I was ready.

Lady Luck smiled on me, and in October, I was told that I had a new date for the surgery in November 2017! This surgery was currently only being done in one city in Canada, and that was Montreal. The surgeon was Dr. Brassard. His is the only private hospital in Montreal, and Dr. Brassard does both plastic surgery and gender affirming surgeries. I learned that the surgery I was about to have was not only hard on the patient but also hard for the surgeon and staff, as there is always a huge risk.

For the presurgery process, I needed blood work, along with other tests, and I was told to stop my hormones at the end of October. After that, I found that my energy was very low, as I was struggling at the gym during my workouts.

I flew to Montreal on November 19, 2017. This was the first time I was so far away from home, alone in the hospital in a strange city, across the country with no family or friends. Although I understood that they couldn't fly due to medical issues or lack of money, I still wished they were there.

When I arrived at the hospital, I was so tired. I ate a bit and met some other women scheduled for surgeries the next day. I wished them all blessings for their surgeries, and then I left to head to bed, even though it was really early.

The following morning, I was afraid and nervous, but I was still there for my fellow patients and able to greet one girl as she was wheeled back into her room after her surgery. Then I was off to see my surgeon for a pre-operation consult.

After that, I met the parents of one of the other girls, and they noticed that I wasn't eating much, due to being a bundle of nerves while waiting for my surgery the following day. They encouraged me to eat a little more if it felt right, and I appreciated their kindness.

My surgery day was November 21, 2017, and I was the first scheduled patient for the day. Still suffering from jet lag, I was so tired walking into the hospital that morning. I completed all the required forms and then had to see the nurses and surgeon one more time before I went in.

The surgery was a success, and although I had some issues, I was well-cared for afterward, even healing so quickly that the surgeons and nurses were shocked at how well I was doing. I believe it was my mindset: get better and you are going to have some fun in life.

After my surgery, the parents I had met—the ones who had encouraged me to eat—came and checked up on me, too. They wished me a speedy recovery, and I felt great knowing that I wasn't alone. When I told them that I had no family or friends with me, they said, "Don't worry. Since *we're* here, we'll give you support while *you're* here." To this day, I still enjoy chatting with them and their daughter on Messenger.

November 23 was my moving day: I had to be moved from the hospital to the recovery house for all transgender surgeries. I was stubborn and wanted to walk into the recovery house, so instead of sitting in the wheelchair, I had to hold onto it while I walked in. I was so lucky that I had my own room near the stairs. I learned the particulars of how my daily life would change postsurgery, which was an adjustment, but I also learned that it gets better each day.

The hospital and recovery house, surgeon, and nurses were amazing—checking on us, making sure we took the prescribed medicines, and recovered well. I had noticed a lot of butterfly pictures in the hospital and in the recovery house, so I asked about them. The staff gently explained that our experience was like going from caterpillar to butterfly. We were caterpillars, and since the surgery, we had turned into pretty butterflies. The nurses were so kind, and the environment in the recovery house was so great.

On November 29, I left Montreal, and it was time to finish my recovery at home in Surrey. I had taken medical leave from work for eleven weeks, which was the longest I'd ever gone without working. Over the next few months, I had to visit a nurse a few times, but I couldn't do much else: no working, no workouts, and no swimming while recovering. It was challenging.

Do I regret this surgery? I would say no, since I feel great and I did a brave thing for my true self. One day, I hope to go back to visit my surgeon and his staff, so I can thank them in person and show them how I've changed since.

A month after the surgery, I saw an ad on Facebook for a grow, evolve, empower women total makeover challenge. I thought, hmm, I'm losing weight and learning to be a better lady; maybe I could do this. I emailed them, asking if they were willing to accept a transgender woman. They said yes, and I applied.

First, I made it into the top thirty, and then the top fifteen. I was so excited. I didn't know much about how to be a woman or what it would be like in a room full of ladies like this. I was also nervous and felt like quitting. My friends in the challenge and the directors and the board all told me to keep it up, and that they were rooting for me as the first transgender woman in the challenge. So, I kept on.

I ended up in the top ten, but I didn't advance beyond that because I had some negative mindsets about myself, and the challenge surfaced some past trauma for me. Still, I'm so glad I did it. The experience was an eye opener and gave me the baby steps I needed to keep moving forward in becoming the true me.

As a result of the challenge, I hired coaches to help me improve my mindset and to heal from my past. Also, I met some amazing ladies in the challenge who have inspired me, and I know we'll be friends forever. Then I went to Parksville, British Columbia, for a self-development conference, and realized that I needed to share my story and that writing a story can help to heal wounds. As one of the authors in this collection, I now have an amazing tribe and support group who can help others and me.

To help me deal with depression as the result of trauma in my past, I've been seeing a counselor, and I've also been going to a church I enjoy. With a more relaxed mindset, I'm excited to be there with open hands and an open heart.

I want to inspire others to enjoy their lives and believe in themselves, to know that they can do anything they want to do. I had to be brave to have the surgery, to participate in a makeover challenge, to go to a conference, to reach out for help, and to write my story for this book. I hope this is a way for people to see what a transgender person is: a person born in the wrong body.

Given how painful and difficult this is, the suicide rate for transgender people is very high, and my goal in life is to help lower this rate by sharing my story. I don't want to see anyone I know have to go through this without support. I want to give others hope and encourage them to get the best help they can. I want other people to know that transgender people have feelings and rights and can work and have fun, just like everyone else. We are all human.

I want you to know that I enjoy my life and I have met amazing people who want to see me shine. I want to see you shine, too, and I thank you for reading my story.

Scars
by Tracy Childs

can't remember why it happened the first time.

I was upset about something, and I know I was crying, but my world at that moment had gone soft. That happens often at stressful moments in life, or because of certain triggers, and my vision softens around the edges. Breathing becomes difficult; moving becomes impossible. When I try to recall the events or feelings afterward, there are always pieces missing.

I don't remember intentionally picking up the razor blade. I don't even know where I got it from, but it was there with me on the bed when the familiar heat of panic rose in my chest and the fuzzy tunnel vision crept in. The tears wouldn't stop, the searing hot hand wrapped around my lungs would not recede, and the endless streams of nasty dialogue in my head would not quiet.

Until it did.

The cuts were slow and shallow at first, the blade sharp enough to sever the nerves so that it didn't even hurt. I was surprised and morbidly fascinated when blood bubbled up through a barely visible separation in my skin. One line turned to two, two to five, and by the time I realized the voices in my head were quiet—a bloody star was clotting on my thigh.

I looked up from the bottom bunk of my childhood bed and saw the room now in amazing hyper focus. A beam of light poured through the crack in my unicorn and rainbow covered curtains, lighting up every speck of dust in its path. Hundreds of tiny suns floated just out of reach; how could I not have noticed them before? The fuzziness was gone. So were the tears and the invisible hand that just moments ago had been squeezing both lungs so hard I really believed I might die. I could think and breathe easily. The only voice left in my head spoke up, clearly and helpfully, "Next time maybe have a towel on hand, so you don't drip on the bedspread. Pressure will stop the bleeding." I liked this voice; it was rational and non-judgmental.

I was fourteen years old at the time, and I thought I had discovered the "cure" for these chronic bouts of paralyzing, spiraling, irrational fear. I hadn't joined a "cutting club" or read about it on the Internet. I didn't know "cutting" and "self-harm" were actually fairly common symptoms of mental distress, and the term "anxiety attack" didn't seem to fully encompass the panic that was always just waiting for a reason to surface. For me, this cathartic bloodletting was a solution, and I had come up with it all on my own.

Knowing what I know now, this was not the first time I had engaged in some form of self-harm—it was just the first time that it seemed to solve a problem.

In my teen years, self-harm became my main coping strategy. It wasn't always cutting, but these behaviours were all part of the same dysfunctional thinking. Harming my body or taking on physical tasks that seemed so ridiculously important (for whatever reason at the time) were glorious distractions from the underlying fear and emotional pain—my body's attempt to control what was going on in my mind. There were times when I refused to eat. There were times I ate and then threw up. There were weeks when I didn't sleep, and then weeks when I did little but.

The months leading up to graduation, and the summer that followed, saw a huge escalation in cuts. My forearms, thighs, and lower legs were covered in parallel lines. The newer ones were still thick with scabs; others had filled in with soft pink flesh. I no longer worried about the nerves or fears or horrible thoughts when they started to escalate, because I always had a hunting knife with me and knew relief from this invisible, emotional pain was just a few drops of blood away.

One night at a friend's barn party, I was curled up in the corner of a horse stall, freaking out (silently, in my head, of course) about what was going to happen in a few weeks when I moved away to college. I cut the side of my calf so deep that I probably should have gone for stitches. Of course, I didn't, so the next day at a horse show, while I smiled my biggest smile and won a big, shiny, red, first-place ribbon—the scab cracked open and my boot filled with blood.

Nobody even knew. Or at least, if they did, they didn't say anything to me. The visible scabs and scars had a bonus side effect of pushing people away. Nobody wants to talk to the crazy girl.

Looking back, I don't know how more people didn't notice. But then, anyone who did happen to ask about my arms seemed content with my standard joke, "I had a fight with a barbed wire fence. I lost."

Even today, thirteen years from my last cut, if someone asks about the scars, I just say, "I got in a fight." If they bother to follow up and ask, "With who?" I say, "Myself."

I've never been able to attempt a real explanation without crying.

Growing up in my family was very quiet. Mostly even silent, unless there was yelling, followed by the silent treatment. Even though we had dinner at the table together every night, we didn't say much. I remember watching my dad—always looking grumpy, staring intensely at the condiments on the table while he ate—and thinking, "What did I do to make him so angry all the time?" In reality, he was probably just running through a to-do list in his head and his expression had nothing to do with me. Or I remember the times I saw my mom hastily wiping away tears from under her glasses when she thought I couldn't see. They were private tears and not meant for me, but for some reason, it hurt that she didn't trust me with them.

With time came a shift in perspective, having my own kids now and dealing with my own struggle of trying to "not look so angry all the time" and "not to cry so much"—I get it. But as a kid, the few times I got up the courage to ask either of my parents what was wrong, the answer I got was always, "Nothing."

So, despite the continually cantankerous or otherwise unhappy body language, I was expected to believe that my parents always had everything well in hand and nothing was ever wrong.

Ever.

So, I stopped asking.

But if nothing was wrong, then why was I so anxious all the time? Dinnertimes became so uncomfortable for me that I employed the strategy of physically hiding. I would wait either outside or in my room until dinner was called, eat as fast and as little as I possibly could, and then disappear for the rest of the night. They didn't seem to miss me. This worked at home and so led to me using the same strategy at school. I was so tired of being called Loser and Fatty, having banana peels thrown at me, and dreading the next time my hair would be lit on fire as I walked down the hall—I started hiding behind the paperback racks in the library until thirty seconds before class, then ran to make it there just in time.

I learned to be silent. I learned to hide. Don't speak up. Don't make waves. Don't draw attention. Definitely don't fail.

Avoidance. Isolation. Self-harm. On some level, knowing these behaviours were wrong only increased the shame. All of which increased the self-harm. Always wanting to be able to tell someone that something was wrong, but never feeling justified that my problems were bad enough to warrant any attention. Terrified that someone would actually know what I was doing to myself. Knowing that the problem was, indeed, myself. I knew I should stop, but these behaviours were helping me get through the day, so why would I?

One of the psychologists I saw over the years was convinced I must have been sexually abused as a child, but I wasn't. Another blamed the school bullying epidemic. Yes, some pretty horrible stuff happened, but I survived. One psychiatrist blamed my parents, and that seemed plausible at the time, but now that I have kids of my own, I realize the amount of parental yelling I experienced as a child was totally justified. Each one agreed there was something wrong with me—some elusive diagnosis that, once pinpointed and medicated, would solve everything and I'd never utilize self-harm again. But none of their therapies or drugs seemed to help much; a Band-Aid doesn't work when the wounds are internal. They had me convinced there must have been some catalyst, some horrific, life-altering event, some reason for me to turn to such behaviour, right?

Nope. Apparently, pain is pain. Whether it's an all at once, massive compound skull fracture from a horrific impact, or the cumulative effects of a thousand forked-tongue paper cuts to your self-esteem, that pain shapes you. That pain made me always some mixture of nervous, scared, or terrified, so it didn't take much to push me over the edge. Physical pain for me was easier to handle than emotional pain, so when the feelings spiraled and became overwhelming, I could always turn to cutting.

It wasn't all completely bleak—there were periods of time in my late teens and early twenties when the fear and the cutting were stifled, and sometimes completely absent. Those times, I have realized, were when I was excited about life instead of dreading it. Times when jobs or relationships were going well and goals were being achieved, when I felt comfortable enough to speak up for myself, and I could see past the circumstances or obstacles and still be excited about what was ahead. But eventually things would change and where I found myself wasn't where I wanted to be anymore. Then the nerves, fears, and panic attacks would reappear and so would the self-harm. But did I speak up, reassess my situation, and head in a different direction?

Of course not.

Nothing was ever allowed to be wrong, because that would mean that everything I had done to get to this point was also wrong. Don't speak up. Don't draw attention. Don't fail. My instinct was always to hide, so why did I continue to resort to this behaviour that left such visible, permanent, obviously self-inflicted, gaping wounds all over my body for everyone to see? The continual conflict between my body and my mind was literally cutting me to pieces.

When I was twenty-five, I met someone who saw my scars and simply said, "Next time, will you tell me what's wrong first?"

Tell someone what was bothering me? Speak up? Actually admit to myself and the world that something was wrong? There was actually someone who wanted to hear about what was in my head? He was probably not the first person to say it, but he was the first one I actually believed wouldn't judge me for anything I said. Maybe it was because I was finally ready to change, and this was the start I needed. I ranted and ranted and ranted to this audience of one, and he encouraged it. He wasn't seeking a diagnosis or label, and he didn't try to fix me. I let thoughts and opinions and problems spill out of my mouth, raw and unfiltered, like blood from a wound, and at first, all he did was listen.

And I never cut again.

I'm not saying the possibility of self-harm is completely gone. Neither are the fears or panic attacks. But somewhere in those first few months of ranting, this person gently talked me back from the edge of panic time after time until I learned how to do it for myself—without the knife. Sometimes, I still find myself reaching for a bottle of alcohol instead of a blade. Sometimes, I'm resisting the impulse to swerve in front of a semi on the highway just to make the pain stop. As long as I recognize that these are self-harming thought processes, as long as I remember that things are allowed to be wrong, I am allowed to speak up, and as long as I understand the anxiety I'm feeling at any given moment means there is something I need to talk about, I will be okay. As long as I choose instead to find someone who will listen to me rant about it, I won't need to cut.

For me, it took blood and scars to lead to talking, which taught me that it's okay for things to be wrong. Whatever it takes to find out what works, and as long as I do it while skin will still heal.

My scars may be ugly and permanent, cause controversy, and draw unwanted attention, but that's okay—because my scars mean that I've survived every battle I've fought against my pain and my fears.

They mean I'm still here.

Power Within
by Holly Holmberg

think before I entered this world, I observed, calculated, and then, turning to the angel next to me, said, "Here, hold my beer. I got this!" I'm sure I felt so strong and ready.

Now, I never truly understand how powerful I am until I find myself standing on the other side of adversity and look back; then it's, "Holy fuck, what a ride!" When I'm in the middle of the adventure, it's hard to see the big picture. Especially during times like the last two years, when it feels like I've already been hit by multiple tsunami waves, and I can see the next one coming.

The only thing that comes to mind are Dory's words from *Finding Nemo*, "Just keep swimming, just keep swimming, swimming, swimming... That's what we do, we like to ssswwiiim!" Gotta love Dory.

August 9, 2016, 9:30 p.m.

My cell phone rings.

It's my mother. "Your brother, Einar, is dead"

"Mom," I say, "that's not funny."

"I'm not joking."

A cold chill runs through me as my heart splits in two, causing a guttural scream of pain to erupt from my body. It travels slowly up over my vocal cords and finally out of my mouth as I drop to my knees. For a brief moment, my world stops.

My brother, five years older than me; my brother, who struggled with a lifelong, painful disease that had left his bones brittle and weak as he aged; my brother, who was my first friend, playmate, mentor, teacher, and hero, died suddenly at fifty-one in our elderly parents' arms while they were performing CPR. The official cause of death stated that he died of pneumonia after having aspirated vomit into his lungs; his vomiting was a reaction to painkillers he received at the hospital for a broken shoulder, caused by a simple fall earlier that morning.

Our family was dropped on its proverbial ass, and we sat dumbfounded, in utter shock. We knew that he would leave us one day, but this was not how we had imagined it. How could someone be so vibrant and full of life at 9:00 a.m. and then dead and gone by 5:30 p.m.? He had plans for that evening; they were left unfulfilled. At least he died with his boots on.

December 16, 2017, 11:30 a.m.

My cell phone rings; it's my son. He is crying, voice panicked, and full of emotion. "Mom, Ashley is on the way to Red Deer in the ambulance. She went into labour seven weeks early. We don't know if the baby is going to be OK—Mom, I can't lose them."

Our grandson, Jackson, was born at1:20 a.m. December 20, weighing in at just over three pounds. A stroke in utero had caused his early birth, and then a second stroke less then twenty-four hours after his birth sent him via stork ambulance to the NICU in Edmonton.

There, he would fight for his life and test the strength of his parents' mental health, their relationship, and support people and systems, plus our family as a whole. Friends and family, both local and worldwide, prayed, sent Reiki, called, and gave us support the best they could, until Jackson was released to go home on February 8, 2018, his original due date.

Jackson is now a healthy six-month old, a giggling, pooping, farting, and wiggling bundle of joy who is showing growth patterns to be a tall, healthy young man and the apple of his family's eye.

December 26, 2017, 5:30 p.m.

My cell phone rings; it's Ashley, my daughter-in-law. "Holly, Jim is gone. He's dead."

My heart stops, that now-familiar chill settles in, and slowly, I feel the cracks as the unscarred areas of my heart start to break apart. Uncertainty sets in as to how my ex-husband's suicide makes me feel—sadness, relief, and pain, lots of pain.

I had just spoken with him on the day of our grandson's birth, urging him to go and see the kids and the baby. He was in a low that only the combination of his depression, the holiday season, and lack of sunlight could take him.

Our twenty-year marriage had ended in 2010 as his mental health had finally taken its toll on our relationship. Since then, he'd lived in a world of regrets, darkness, and pain that we could not reach through; his first attempt at suicide had been foiled three years earlier by a quick response of a longtime family friend. Jim truly believed no one could help him with his mental health, so he wouldn't do any form of therapy or mental work to help himself. He was only interested in taking his prescription medication; he wanted a miracle pill that would just snap him out of it.

Now the reality hits that the father of my children has succeeded in taking his life at a time when our daughter, son, and grandson need him most. Christmas, a time that has already proved to be a dreaded holiday in our family, is now officially blown clear off the calendar and burned into our psyche as a dark time. My fury starts to burn, glowing like a volcano quaking for a Plinian explosion of rage.

My thoughts switch to my children, and my rage shifts to a mother's grief as I think back to yesterday, Christmas day, when I held our son, his twenty-three-year-old body curled up in my lap like he was five. He was grieving, in pain and fear for his baby, on life support in the NICU, begging to just be able to hold him in his arms and take him home. At the moment, my boy is a two-hour drive away from me, alone with his new family and the weight of the world on his shoulders. My basic mothering instinct makes me only want to be there to hold and comfort him in his time of need and tragedy, and I'm unable to. Worse yet, I think, "What if Jackson doesn't pull through?" I can't think of that.

Thoughts shift to our daughter, as the vehicle I'm in hurls down the highway to get me to her side. She spent the last two years of her life flirting with the idea of suicide as an end to her war with depression, anxiety, and PTSD. How is she going to react to this news of her father's suicide? Their relationship was tension-filled at best, plus they hadn't seen or spoken to each other in months. Is she going to hang onto her tender mental health or crash into her grief and depression, potentially following in her father's footsteps, causing us to lose her too? Would I be ready for that if she did?

Am I ready for the storm of emotion and pain that is about to erupt and flow from my babies for the next steps that we all have to take, knowing that we had no choice but to move forward into an uncharted future?

How dare he hurt our children in this way—they needed him, we needed him.

April 16, 2018

After a year-and-a-half battle, a childhood friend of forty years dies of cancer, despite the natural healing support that I had offered, as well as numerous medical treatments; it is hard to watch your friend slowly die.

I numbly deliver her eulogy and talk of how I, as a young girl, used to help change her diapers.

April 16, 2018

At my friend's funeral, I learn from my mother that my dad is in the hospital. He had his fifth stroke and has lost partial use of his right side. I stop at the hospital after the funeral to visit with him; he is positive and in good spirits. I leave and start the three-hour drive for home, plenty of time for me to digest the events of the day.

I am getting tired of people dying and me being strong. I want to curl up in a ball and hide.

May 2, 2018

My eighty-seven-year-old father has a major stroke; we are uncertain if he is going to come home. I would have thought that his years of battling a heart condition, bypass surgery, minor heart attacks, and previous strokes would have hardened and prepared me for his inevitable passing, but it doesn't. He is placed into palliative care.

His will to live and keep going is overwhelming, amazing even to his doctor. Dad is removed from palliative care after being put there less than twenty-four hours prior. His pneumonia clears, and he's up and walking with his walker, begging to go home.

This stroke has taken most of his speech, energy, and ability to walk on his own; it's caused incontinence and scrambled some of his thoughts. After a two-week stay in the hospital, Mom gets to take him home.

To watch a strong, six-foot-tall virile Viking of a man—one who, in his prime, used to bring Volkswagen Beetles into the dance hall as a practical joke—slowly fade has been the hardest of all.

Now, the first man I ever loved, heart and soul, is dying before my eyes. I am grateful for the last days together, but I ache as I watch him slowly weaken, a beautiful, strong soul trapped in a body that no longer serves him. My worst nightmare plays out before me.

True to his tenacious nature, Dad still sneaks out of the house and away from my mother's watchful eagle-like gaze to hill the potatoes in the garden, mow the lawn, or shuffle down to his beehives to check on his beloved apiary, which he has kept for the past seventy-four years. As funny as it is, it stresses the crap out of Mom.

I wonder if she's going to survive this or will I lose them both? My eldest brother hardly talks to me as he battles his own grief over the circumstances we face. We were once so close, but now I feel as if I have lost him too.

My soul whispers, "Don't think that. Move on. Take the next step and see the light in the dark. You don't need to see the whole path, just the next step. Keep moving forward."

Every time Dad and I part, I hug him tightly and cry inside. His arms no longer have the strength to hold me as they once did when I was so little and scared, but at least he can still hug me. I see the love and tears in his eyes as we part; he is very emotional these days as we all know the final day is coming. Our hunting days are already done, but soon, one day, there will be no more knowing looks, no more soft teasing in Norwegian, and worst of all, no more hugs.

August 2018

I find it truly amazing that my heart can still beat through all this pain and grief. I guess what keeps it going is those flashes of beauty and awe amongst the pain. The little miracle of love when I look into the eyes of my now six-month-old grandson as he giggles at the silly faces I make, the soft teasing of my father, or how he skillfully sharpens my butchering knives and keeps me company as I cut and wrap the quarter of beef we just bought from a local farmer, Dad still instructing me on what cuts to make to ensure a tender meal in the days to come.

I know that there is always beauty, even in the pain; I just need to breathe and look around my current story to see the big picture and marvel at the lessons. To understand that strength and power come from within me, from the teachings of my parents, loved ones now passed on, and my life experiences.

I know that I never get handed more than I can take, even though some of these hellish days are worse than others. I know to look for the shortcuts and not stop to sit in a pity party, for it will not move me forward on my journey. Although hard at times, this journey also teaches me to be strong, soft, and supple. To above all remain vulnerable and allow the river of pain to flow from me rather than damming it up and allowing it to fester into an internal poison for my soul.

I have learned that to truly love and experience all that life has to offer, I cannot hold back. I have to remain malleable, vulnerable, and open to love and trust, acknowledging that I may get hurt or even broken by doing so. This malleability is what keeps me supple and strong like a willow tree, bending and flowing with the forces of nature. And those cracks and breaks in my heart and soul are mending in time with the gold solder of experience and lessons learned, making my heart and soul a beautiful sight to behold.

I have learned to take action and forge a new path, leaning hard into it, to create the opportunities I want. I also know to make necessary changes along the way, honoring the fact that I, and those who have touched my life, in ways good, bad or ugly, are only human. Forgiving them, but mostly forgiving myself. Never forgetting the trespasses, but instead cutting their chains to me and leaving them in the past as building blocks for my future.

Living life to the fullest so when that day comes and I meet them all again, I can show that I chose love over fear and slide in sideways, grabbing my beer from that patient angel, and saying, "Wow! What a ride, for I have truly lived!"

As I Speak My Truth
by Laura-Lee Harrison

I had just finished work for the night at a local bar where I had been bartending for a couple months. A friend was hanging out with me while I worked, and we had met some cute boys who invited us to their cabin for an after party. We accepted their invitation and went with them to their cabin. When we arrived, one of the guys opened the fridge and it had rose-colored homemade wine in it. He popped the cork and poured us some wine. The taste was fruity as the bubbles filled my mouth upon first sip. Delicious.

We all decided to go for a walk in this magical area around the cabin. I was completely in awe. I had no idea this area existed within this tiny town in British Columbia. I remember the cabin was surrounded by these stunning old moss-covered trees. I could hear the relaxing trickle and bubble of the creek beside us. The area was thick, and the trees seemed gigantic, but I could still see the beautiful star-ridden sky. The fresh summer air hit my nose with the woodsy smell combined with my fruity, homemade blush wine. The wind just ever so slightly rustled the trees, and I clearly remember admiring the absolute beauty I was walking through. I found a fallen tree and sat with one of those cute boys. As we talked and flirted a little, I could see and hear my friend with the other guy, laughing and talking in the short distance in front of us, toward the cabin. The light on the deck shined behind her head. What a captivating evening and space to be in.

At this point, I had only had a few drinks from the wine provided. I had been sober from being at work all night. As this man's arms came around me and he started to make moves on me, I very distinctly said, "No, I'm not interested in hooking up tonight, and I have my period right now."

I woke up the next morning on my stomach and very clearly had someone on top of me. The first thing I thought was, "Where am I?" and, "Oh, no! I must have decided to say yes, even though I'm on my period. Gross!" I was a little baffled and dazed, but I was sure I must have agreed to it, so I didn't think too much of it.

After the haze lifted slightly and I could see straight, I collected my things and my friend and I said goodbye, hugged the guys, and left. We went for breakfast. Feeling absolutely dreadfully sick, I had the worst headache of my life. We started talking to piece the night together, and she shared with me her experience, which was basically the same as mine.

When I sat down at the table at the restaurant for breakfast, the shocking pain I experienced was absolutely intense. I very clearly hadn't realized until this point that I had more than just vaginal sex the night before. This was a not a comfortable feeling at all; this is something I would never agree to and had never experienced prior. I was extremely hungover, or so I thought, and due to that, for a long time, I never gave another thought to what had happened in its entirety.

My attitude was that it is done, move on, I cannot do anything now, and I know nothing about this guy. I wasn't sure I could even find the cabin again if I tried. I had a lot of blame in my head and shame that I brought on myself. I shouldn't have gone to the cabin. I should not have drank their drinks. I know better than to take drinks from strangers. I really did not want anyone to know about what had happened to me at all. My friend and I never even talked about it, other than over breakfast that next morning. I've always had a feeling she did not want to speak of it. Though that is not a fair assumption, it is an uncomfortable topic to talk about. Maybe it was purely me who did not wish to speak about it.

A couple of months later, I was at the bar working, and the guy, the "cute boy" from that night I'd tried to forget, walked in alone and started hitting on me. At this point, I hadn't fully pieced together that I had been drugged and raped by him, but I also felt icky and ashamed. Being someone who didn't like confrontation and wasn't super secure with my instincts, I served him, and I allowed him to be there.

Eventually, he got belligerent and was refusing to pay. I came out from behind the bar to talk to him and my boss, who was drunk, came at me and verbally attacked me, calling me a whore and a slut. She told me, in words I don't care to repeat, that I needed to take my sexual escapades outside of the bar at the end of the night and get back to work. This type of aggression toward me was out of character for her, however was not surprising. Her family had just gone through a loss of a loved one and inherited the bar. I felt the owners were all under a lot of stress with the takeover. Since then, I have forgiven her; we've talked and stayed in touch over the years.

On that night, however, I walked away from both my boss and my rapist, crushed that, while I was being honorable and asking for payment from him, she humiliated me and allowed him to treat her employee that way. He then went and hung out with some customers in the bar and proceeded to tell them some stories about me, I assume, to get under my skin.

Fortunately for me, and unfortunately for him, the men he was talking with were people I had gone to high school with in another town that just so happened to walk into the bar that night, unexpectedly. They took control of the situation and kicked him out of the bar for me. These guys knew me well enough that they refused to tell me what he said, and they knew what he was saying was not true.

All of this happened eleven years ago, and honestly, I didn't know or understand the effect that this incident had on me until recently. It took me years to realize that I had even been date raped.

After realizing I indeed was date raped by this man, I have experienced shame put upon me by others. This has likely been more damaging than the actual rape. Because of the rape, I have experienced intimacy issues, such as not allowing men into my life or heart. I have often felt that if it is going to be taken from me with no regard to my wellbeing physically, mentally, and emotionally, then why bother getting close with anyone, or ever standing my ground and saying no again?

When I've experienced what I thought to be love, I chose to take that step toward intimacy to create the deeper connection by sharing my voice and my truth. I had hoped I would find safety where I had once lost it, which was a very frightening step to take. Fear of being ridiculed and blamed often held me back from speaking about what happened to me. What felt like knots in my throat would stop me from forming any kind of words! After I decided it was time, it often took me days, if not months, to actually speak up. Unfortunately, when the time finally came, the knots had loosened just a little, and I was able to choke the words out, I actually did end up experiencing my exact fears: tremendous amounts of shame and abuse, hate, and ultimate blaming.

"Slut."

"Whore."

"You did something to deserve it."

"You asked for it."

"You shouldn't have been drunk."

"How could you let that happen to you?"

"You're disgusting."

"You're diseased now."

Every time I heard these words, it destroyed me. It made me feel like I was unworthy of love and healthy relationships, and that it wasn't safe to tell anyone, especially men, about my experience. This also had a ripple effect on other areas of my life. I still experience that knot in my throat from time to time, specifically when I have to speak my truth to someone and I perceive it may be a difficult conversation to have. As I move through those types of conversations and use my voice, the knot gets smaller, and it has become easier to express myself over time. However, now that I am looking at it with new eyes, the impact the experience had on me and the influence on my relationships through the years is actually very profound.

Recently, I was in a relationship, and considering speaking up about my past to my boyfriend caused me to go into a fear ridden space. The knot. I had a hard time expressing myself, and I felt my past was way too much for him. It definitely caused anxiety for me and issues between us. I was completely unaware of why this was happening. He is a good man, and he treated me very well—he was super supportive and believed in me. He also knew bits and pieces of my past but no details. I had never had any negative reactions from him, and he told me often how strong I was. Still, I could not bring myself to speak my truth to him in its entirety. I felt safe with him and safe to confide in him, so why was this an issue for me?

I sat with it. I confided in a friend. I wondered, what is causing me to clam up and not speak to this man and ultimately, to push him away with my silence? One morning, a day or so after this conversation, I was doing my goddess yoga. The warm, spring sun gleamed through my window onto my back while I was in child's pose, and it came to me: I have fear of sharing any part of myself with this wonderful man, who I truly love, because all I have experienced in my past has been pain and blame. I have subconsciously believed it is not safe for me to share my darkness.

This man has been a huge part of my success and moving forward in both my emotional life and my entrepreneurial life. Although our romantic relationship ended, we remained friends. To this day, I still have not shared my ultimate truth with him. I don't, however, believe I need to. I do not feel I will find safety by telling him. Instead, I have found the safety I was previously looking for within myself. We were on different paths when we met, and I wholeheartedly believe he was meant to enter my life to be a transition, part of my movement forward in realization and healing. If this relationship would not have happened, I may not have decided to share this part of my life within the pages of this book.

I believe that not being able to speak up kept recurring for me because I had something to learn about my voice. Finally, it was time to let myself know—and time to let that young, twenty-year-old me know—that maybe I could have made different choices that night, but ultimately I did nothing wrong.

I did not ask to be drugged and raped by this "cute" boy.

I did not deserve to be humiliated, shamed, or guilted by people I loved.

I am not a whore.

I am not a slut because someone took my choices away.

I had already voiced my choice when I said no.

There is no excuse for a person to take another human being's choice away. There is no excuse for another person to shame a victim of rape.

Writing this piece is my way of allowing freedom to my darkness that has had power over my relationship with myself and with others. I release the shame of someone else's actions done to me eleven years ago. I stand proud that I have been given a voice, one that will never be knotted up and choked on with fear again.

Look at Me
by Marta Clay

Moments after giving birth by cesarean section, my eyes locked with Kurtis's, and my immediate thought was, "He already knows more than I will know in my lifetime."

From the first day home, I found that when a certain commercial came on the television, the sound had to be muted. Because, if it wasn't, he would wake up from a deep sleep.

After the third round of immunizations, Kurtis changed. My normally engaged baby became distant, and I found it hard to capture his attention. I'm not saying the serums caused the change, but, I believe it was the catalyst for the change. Being a first-time mom, I was concerned about that change but thought it was possibly a phase Kurtis was going through, not realizing that this was a permanent shift.

At six months of age, Kurtis knew what a McDonald's billboard was and would only point to those, and say, "D." His first words were "cracker" and "outside," not "mama" and "daddy."

When he did say "daddy," I tried hard to get him to say "mama." I would coax him with "say mama," but instead, he would say "dah-dah." I finally put two-and-two together. I asked Kurtis to say "daddy," and he said "dah." Then I asked him to say "mama," and he said "dah-dah." The mystery was solved. He had been calling out to both of us, but not in traditional terms.

At one year old, Kurtis knew his alphabet by sight—both uppercase and lowercase, although not the alphabet song. His dad would sit with Kurtis in his lap, at night, and look at the flexible, soft plastic book made for teething babies. On the back cover was the alphabet; Kurtis would point to the letters, one at a time, and his dad would tell him what he was pointing to. One night, I realized, that his dad was doing the pointing, and Kurtis was telling him the letters. I was shocked and delighted at this revelation. What did I have on my hands with this child?

By eighteen months, Kurtis could spell his whole name—first, middle, and last. He could count to one hundred in English and to twenty in Spanish, thanks to *Dora the Explorer*. At this point, he was reading at a first-grade level, and I learned that he also had a photographic memory. Kurtis could watch an episode of *Blue's Clues* and do the whole show again for me, exactly as it was presented on television. I was in awe of such a memory for someone so young.

My husband, Don, came into our lives, when Kurtis was five. Don was a former classroom school teacher. He said, "Kurtis is the smartest kid I have ever met but is socially immature for his age."

I loved that Don could see Kurtis's strengths as well as his challenges. At this point in my life, I needed the support and guidance of a partner who would be involved in Kurtis's care, and love him as much as I did. With the business Don had built and the resources it provided, we could do whatever was necessary to help Kurtis attain a remarkable quality of life with no limitations. It afforded me the opportunity to focus entirely on Kurtis, travel extensively, expose him to countless adventures, and never have to gain permission to do such things. Unconditional love, support, and freedom as I have never known was what Don offered to me. I was so relieved, delighted, and grateful.

The same year, an agent in our office was having issues passing a continuing education exam in life insurance. We had spent hours working with her, and the evening was growing late. Kurtis, who was five at the time, sat down at the desk, which made him appear ever-so-much smaller, and began to take the online exam. Within thirty minutes, he had passed with an 80 percent, and everyone could go home. It was amazing to witness Kurtis accomplish such a task.

When Kurtis was six, he came home from school and wanted to learn multiplication. So, we started teaching him the concepts, and, of course, he mastered it quickly.

Although I marveled at his intellect, I didn't always have an easy time with my son. I would get irritated because Kurtis wouldn't look at me when I was talking to him. I would scold him and say, "Look at me when I'm talking to you. You haven't heard a word I've said." He would then proceed to repeat, word for word, what I had said. I didn't know he couldn't look at me and pay attention to what I was saying. Later, I realized that if he looked at me, trying to read my facial expression and what mood I was in would garner all of his attention.

When I would take Kurtis to the office, I would tell him to just answer people's polite questions and let them go to the tasks they needed to do. But, that was never the case. He would tell them everything known to man about dinosaurs for extended periods of time. People found him fascinating and loved to hear his encyclopedia-like dissertation. But, I thought he was being a disobedient child because he totally ignored my instructions. He also talked at people, not with them.

From an early age, and for my sanity, Kurtis needed a schedule that was consistent. For me, this could sometimes be hard to cope with, but in the grand scheme of things, it made life easier. I learned, by all means, do not tell him a certain time that anything was supposed to happen, because there would be a meltdown because of it. He would ask me every morning for a detailed listing of the day's event. And, heaven forbid that his bath time was not on schedule.

Kurtis was diagnosed at nine with Asperger's syndrome. This explained a lot of what his idiosyncrasies were about, and how we were already making allowances to make life easier to cope with on a daily basis. Once I understood what this actually meant, I was excited to know his peculiarities had a name. However, shortly after the diagnosis, he wanted to commit suicide because he was being bullied relentlessly at school. I was heartbroken and angry that children could be so ruthless and uncaring toward another person. My initial reaction was to get these children punished. Soon, I realized they were not my concern. Kurtis needed my reassurance and guidance to navigate his feelings.

I removed Kurtis from public school at the end of fifth grade and homeschooled him until his graduation at age sixteen. I did this for two major reasons—he was being bullied mercilessly, and because of different types of therapies that would have him out of the classroom several afternoons a week, which would be frowned upon.

Therapies or techniques that we have utilized are: occupational therapy, animal-assisted therapy, EMDR (eye movement desensitization and reprocessing), hippotherapy, listening therapy, social skills classes, psychologists, acupuncture, and fire bottles.

Through all the therapy sessions, I learned that, as a mom, there were no lengths I would not go to help Kurtis. And, as a human being, there have been many times that I wanted to quit, find a corner, and suck my thumb. But, God has given me the honor and privilege of raising Kurtis, and it has been my duty to teach him how to be a caring and responsible adult. The ultimate satisfaction has been seeing him grow into such a fine individual with a keen empathy toward others, and not being afraid to speak out when others have been done wrong.

As a person, I have always strived to look inside others to see their value and not rate them on one episode in their life. It is extremely hard when people are being abusive to your child, and all you want is the situation to be seen as you perceive it and to understand why it is important to you.

My education regarding people has had its low moments, but I still know that we are on this earth for a purpose, and my goal is to help people see that our differences are not a detriment, but an asset to us all. No matter how dour a circumstance may appear, there is a nugget of gold, if you choose to look for it.

Look at me and know that love, understanding, and perseverance will prevail over all obstacles that are in your way.

My First Step in Healing Begins
by Wendy Walsh

Where does a person begin their story? Do you go back as far as your memory will allow? How can you remember all the good and ignore and bypass all the ones you've tried so hard to forget and suppress so deep inside?

Well, here and now, I'm not going to ignore those darker, deeper memories of my past and meet them face to face, up real close and personal. As hard and scary as this is for me, I hope they become less painful as I write. And maybe, just maybe, my words will help someone else to find their strength to begin their process of healing.

I remember always feeling like I never really belonged to my family. I could have sworn I was adopted because I was so different in personality, looks, and emotions from everybody in it. I grew up with an older brother and sister (seven and six years respectively), and I recall being told and made to feel like a burden to them. I was told I was a brat, a nuisance, and just a pain in the ass. I felt I never really fit in or had a place to feel like I belonged or was accepted. I believe this is where my insecurities and depression started to rise to the surface and become a daily occurrence in my life, became a part of who I was then, and shaped who I am now.

I grew up feeling lonely and different. Honestly, I don't even remember having any real friends growing up. So, when I did get attention from someone, a potential friend, it made me happy. It felt good to be liked and have somebody who wanted to play with me.

When I was around eight years old, my mom started to work full time, my dad was off working, and my brother and sister weren't around, so I had to go to the neighbors' to wait until someone was home. This, as I now have come to realize, is one of those memoires I chose to bury deep down. They were neighbors that had been around for years. All of us kids went to the same school, moms and dads would say, "Hi," and chitchat like neighbors do. But we never really spent any time together as friends; we were just neighbors.

I remember having a "weird" feeling about the dad—a feeling of not trusting him and never wanting to be around him, especially alone. The daughter, Paula, was the one who I would be spending my time with while I waited for someone to come home. On one occasion, Paula and I were horsing around in the basement of their place when she said, "Hey, let's play under the stairs." I thought, OK, sure; it seemed like a good idea. There were lots of blankets and pillows and even a sheet hanging to cover the opening to this spot under the stairs. It was dark, as she had turned the lights off before we crawled in.

I don't recall the words she said to me, but I remember her wanting to pull my pants and underwear down so she could touch me. As she pulled them down and started to touch my vagina, I felt so confused and scared, and I couldn't move. I knew she was talking, but I couldn't hear what she was saying because my own voice in my head was yelling at me to get up, move, say no, you don't like this. I couldn't speak or move my legs or arms, I just laid there listening to my inside voice yelling. Eventually, after what felt like hours but in reality it was probably only minutes, I finally found the strength to roll over, pull up my pants and underwear, and tell her I was going outside. I left as fast as my wobbly legs could go. I went and sat on the steps of my house experiencing thoughts and feelings I didn't know what to do with or how to deal with. So much confusion in my little mind. I was scared and sad at the same time. What just happened and what did I do? Did I do something wrong? Why would she do that to me? I was an eight-year-old little girl who just experienced sexual assault by another little girl. How could she wrap her eight-year-old naïve brain around such a thing?

How would she say anything to her mom and dad about this, and God forbid, to her brother or sister? So, the anxiety, the negative thoughts, all the insecurities, and depression started growing their roots.

I refused to go to the neighbors' after that day, and the reason was never really talked about. I just remember asking, and somehow convincing, my mom for my own house key and telling her that I could stay by myself until someone got home. I would be OK by myself for such a short period of time. And I never went back to the neighbors'—ever.

I avoided them as best as I could from then on, until one day, they moved. I'm not sure how I felt that day, I don't recall, but I bet I let out a huge sigh of relief knowing that I wouldn't have to keep my distance and always be on the lookout for them.

The incident could now be placed in that deep, dark place in your brain where these kinds of unpleasant memories live. Hopefully never to be thought of again. Fingers crossed. Ignore it, and it will go away, right?

I never told anyone this happened to me, until one day, on a nice walk in a park with a very close and dear friend, I told her. We had been chatting about what I would write my chapter about for the *Sacred Hearts* book. As we sat at the picnic table, the sun shining, and our dogs playing, I just let it all out. It felt odd speaking out loud about this, as I never had spoken about it, ever.

I decided then that I needed to write this secret down and let it go. I carried this burden for far too many years. And as I wrote, it just felt, I don't know, like the curtains opened and the room became full of sunlight and I could see.

It's obvious to me now that that one incident deeply affected that little girl I was then.

And how Paula must have been doing to me what she had done to her—and I'm going to venture a guess that it was done by her father. Those gut feelings I had experienced about him back then made so much sense to me now. I feel sick to my stomach and sad for Paula with this realization. I now wonder what she must have gone through all those years ago, and I hope she survived it all.

And now, as a forty-nine-year-old woman, I am finally letting go of that memory that I carried and felt so much shame about. I can now release all that sadness and shame that little eight-year-old me felt, let her know it was never her fault, and she is OK! *We* are OK!

In Heaven
by Nancy (Nance) Chaplin

have something for you. Can I come by?" My eyes see the text, and I set down the phone. Tears touch my eyes, and my heart speaks to hers. Her spirit sees my spirit, we connect through time and all dimensions. My friend—the one who does Reiki, the one I can be real with. I'm on the deck full of mourners, for her. I'm avoiding talking to them. I don't want to be here. I'm on the edge of falling apart.

I long to scroll through my text messages to find the source, the root, the answer. Could this text from my friend possibly be the message I prayed for? Would they send me the answers in a text message? I am expecting, wanting, and demanding a divine answer. I am not brazen enough to ask for JC himself or the trumpet call of Gabriel. Seriously, how can I know if this is the answer? Is this a promise or a punishment, and what do I deserve?

My hands shake, I twitch and reach for my phone again. The flashback of my carpet-crawling crack days—seeking, searching, longing for that one piece of relief—taunt and tempt me. I long to reach for that one small, addictive nugget; one small, toxic crumb; one small, delightful demon of candy. I would do anything, almost anything, to escape the mad hamster wheel of my mind. The constant cycle of growing grief is sucking, smothering, and suffocating each precious memory from me. I hunger to search the memories of my mind, drawer by drawer, for the missing piece of the puzzle, the pattern, and the answer to the why. Candy doesn't help though, and candy leads to one and then another until the entire eight ball is inhaled.

I've loved candy since I was a child. Melt-in-your mouth candy—teeny tiny green mints, golden brown bubbly, spongy succulence, and sweet cinnamon hearts. Name a candy, any candy, and my mouth waters. The sweet relief of happiness wrapped in honey, maple, cane sugar, brown sugar. I'm not picky. Any kind of sugar will suffice. I ache for the escape. I thirst to transcend the pain. Just one taste, just one hit. "She always had a sweet tooth." My mother's truth and my unspoken shame.

I surrender my soul to my breath and stay in the pain, here deep in the furthest corner of the deck. Meditate, don't medicate is my mantra as I choose to stay in the present moment and not escape. Oceans and lakes of saltwater damned, hidden behind hazel-green eyes. Never let them see the pain. If you start crying, you will not be able to stop the floodgates. Just breathe, you've got this kiddo. I'm right here with you. I always have been. I close my eyes, find my Drishti, soften my gaze, and relax my shoulders. The weight of my world begins to slowly waterfall down my spine.

Blood red rivers of pain. Mandarin orange balls of tortured, trapped, wretched, pitiful humiliation. Sunflower-yellow sharp crystal flowers of ineffective, feeble procrastination. My breath escorts them into the gates of Gaia and opens my heart to a garden. I seek refuge in the garden of my delight and demise. I come here often for the salve of my saviour where we walk together in the garden. Concrete, iron-will walls strategically built around the castle. I suppress my sobbing soul and focus my falcon gaze upon the distant aquamarine mermaid waters. Cotton candy clouds surround me. I breathe and inhale deeply into decade deep scars. I feel and see purple hope on the horizon. Glittering, golden, grace-filled lavender clouds rain down and wash with their warmth. I stay in the delightful golden glitter until I feel a blissful, calm trust. My beauty-filled eyes softly open, and I see the water. Her beauty keeps me there, and I see beyond the blood stains on the dock. I know she's here. I just have to find her. Connect with her sweet soul and know that she's okay.

Peace and quiet, hope and patience are the wings upon which I find my strength. My wings are broken. I have reached the sky. Until we meet again, my baby fly.

When I open my eyes, I ignore the massing mount of mourners to the best of my abilities.

"I don't know how she does it."

"How does she keep it all together?"

I hear them and I do not acknowledge them. Suffer for the children, eat the pain, keep it all in, and nothing will remain. I am the strong, silent mother. Blood dripping as I bite my tongue and swallow the pain-filled bile. Spitting is not lady like. Allowing the undigested pain-filled scalloped potatoes and honey-glazed ham from last night's dinner to escape Linda Blair style is not an option.

I reach for my phone and ignore the empty heart-filled messages of love. I cannot acknowledge them or the loss until I know she is safe. Safe in the arms of the son of God who tore her from my world. How could you take her from me? We were not finished yet! We had so many plans! We were going to go to college together. I was going to be there with her when my granddaughter and grandson were born; we were going to live and love and dance. We made a pinky swear, a double pinky swear—live like it is heaven here on earth. How can I possibly live on this earth without her? How could the man I trusted the most take you from me? Why didn't he close the pearly gates and leave you here with me?

My Helen Keller hands feel the phone that I have forgotten I am holding. I remember the message from my friend, the one who gets it. I need her here. Numb, dumb, deaf hands respond, "Yes please. Hurry! I'm losing my shit. I can't hold on much longer."

Moment by moment, breath by breath, I survive. I gaze in wonder at the man across the room as he holds my gaze, my heart, and my trust. He brings to me what I need now in this moment—nicotine and caffeine. He whispers in my ear the words I need to know, "I'm going to the hospital, honey. I'll stay with him. Call me if you need me." His strength leans in and kisses my wet cheek, with the softness of her lips, and she whispers, "I love you." My knight in shining armour and his queen. I am proud to be a daddy's girl because I am strong, tenacious, and heaven bent—I'm finding my joy. My father taught me to be strong and stand up for myself through years of addiction, abuse, and codependency. Strong enough to handle anything except what we could never imagine.

Emily Joy Chaplin died on August 26, 2011. Two days after my father's birthday. She called him that day and he didn't answer. She sang him "Happy Birthday" and left a message on his phone. He listens to it every year and misses her. We all do. We will remember her joy, for she truly lived a lifetime in ten sweet years. A tragic boating accident they called it. A no-fault accident. They took blood from my son, a battered boy, whose shoulder was filled with shrapnel, whose patella was smashed, and whose spine was twisted. The driver swerved to avoid what appeared to be an abandoned Sea-Doo. Witnesses called us and reached out—excessive speed, erratic driving—and we told the police. They investigated the crime and interrogated my son. Yet they took no blood from the boat driver—they deemed it unnecessary.

My friends hung a banner on his dock and scattered rose petals in the water. We wanted him to know what we had lost. Gone but not forgotten, forever in our hearts, and always on our minds. "Family first" is our creed, and my sons adorned their bodies with solid black ink to always remember.

"Quitters never win, and winners never quit."
"Say what you mean. Mean what you say. And don't say it mean."

These are the words she left us with. Words we taught each other.

One cigarette, two cigarettes, three cigarettes, and she appears. She doesn't ask me how I'm doing. She's a true friend, a chosen sister, and she knows better. Her radiant Reiki hands surround my soul, my heart, and my entire body. I always feel better when she's around. Her presence brings a calm, peaceful light into the dark abyss of my pain. Her offering, her gift, is twofold.

"I have a message for you," she says. "It's in a picture on your computer. They only gave me two words: In Heaven. Honey, do you remember the picture?" I know she means her spirit guides. What I don't know is what started shaking first—my hands or my head. "No, no, no, I don't remember. I don't remember a damn thing. That's the problem! It's all gone, all my memories. I'm afraid of losing my mind."

My sister by design keeps the mongrel mass of mourners away from me with a tray full of fruit. I must hold them at bay until I'm ready to be the mother, daughter, and wife I must be. The strong one, the one who has it all together, and who is falling apart at the seams. I know she has my back, and I trust her. Trust is something new. An itchy plaid sweater that feels tight around my neck. A sweater I am, nevertheless, willing to wear. Just for today.

We scour the pages of Facebook together to find the picture. The mourners disappear as minutes turn into hours, and we find "the one." A beautiful picture of the lake that is before me. A simple caption below, "In Heaven." I sigh, knowing she is home, and yet I still feel her here with me.

Days before my daughter died, she asked me if we could stay in Kelowna. I smiled and replied, "One day, sweetie, one day, sweetie, just not yet. I promise, double pinky swear that we'll come back and be together forever and ever and live happily ever after."

The second fold of my friend's gift introduced me to Emily's new friends—Michael, Metatron, Gabriel, Uriel, and Raphael. She told me they were with her now. *Messages from Your Angels* was the first book of many whose healing words brought me connection and comfort in the lonely days ahead without my best friend. There is not one single day that I don't think of her. Her brothers and I share stories of her sweet, sassy, spunky determination as we continue to heal from the pain of her loss and learn the lessons on our paths.

I walked through the days following her passing praying to the God I both hated and adored, for the strength to hold my head up high and honour her memory. Her father and I grew miles and mountains apart as I healed. Our journey ended when we lost our Joy, and soon our marriage followed course. "I love you, but I am not in love with you," were the words I heard when he told me our marriage was over. A sentiment and truth I knew years and years before. I stayed the course in my healing, like I did in our tumultuous, painful marriage, for the same reason—I had to take care of my children.

Staying strong for them was easy, until I fell apart. Each one came to my side like warrior princes and held my hand, my heart, and my soul. Their words of encouragement—"You've got this, Mom. You know you can do it, and I am proud of you"—became my mantras. The same words I had told them became the words I heard from them when my strength wavered. It wavered often.

I learned to take the difficult, daunting days of firsts moment by moment and breath by breath. Each birthday and holiday without her was a deep, blood-soaked pain that I endured with the help of true family and friends.

I took the hard road to healing and cowered under the cover of codependency, caring more about my children and ex-husband than I did about myself. I healed from codependency, layer by layer through my studies of yoga, meditation, Reiki, emotional freedom technique (EFT), angel card readings, aromatherapy, Bach remedies, and addiction.

I learned the exponential power of my emotions and the laws of the universe. I continue to master the processes of each healing medium and practice them myself daily to stay in the light, as I continue to heal from the pain of loss, betrayal, and abuse. Layers and layers of repressed memories unfold daily—a traumatic childhood, adolescence, and a destructive, abusive marriage.

Three years later, I met the man of my dreams, and together, we have formed a bond that grows stronger each day. Our healing is a sacred part of our journey. Our emotions are our guides, and we learn from each other every day.

I am no longer governed by the painful presence of post-traumatic stress disorder (PTSD). I have learned that we are all souls wrapped in disguises. The mask I once wore to hide the abuse has been shed, and I now talk openly about the grace-filled experiences that brought me from trauma to triumph.

My joy is truly exponential, and I wake each day with arms wide open to the grace of the experiences and opportunities that spirit brings to me.

Learning to Be Courageous One Lesson At a Time
by Stephanie Leach

As the young woman thought about her life, she was excited to be moving forward into a new chapter marrying the man she loved. At twenty-five, she was ready to live a perfect life with her husband and the children they would one day have. Tonight was the eve of her wedding, and this woman—my mother had just one night left as a single woman.

As usual, her stepfather had been drinking. He threatened to hit her and ruin her wedding day, but she was having none of it. She said, "You get away with beating Mom, but if you lay a hand on me, you will be in jail."

He backed down, probably because he could see in his stepdaughter's eyes that her anger and pent up anxiety simmered below the surface and was ready to explode.

She could never understand why her mom stayed with a man who hurt her so badly when he was drinking. Maybe it was that he was a wonderful man when he was sober. How could she stay with him when she was the breadwinner who brought up her three children who were scared every day about what might happen next? Perhaps she did she not realize the emotional abuse they were enduring. Or was she too wrapped up in her own limiting beliefs to believe she was worthy of a better man and better life?

Maya Angelou said, "When you know better, you do better." Although Mom desperately wanted a different outcome, she continued the cycle of abuse. As I got older, I somehow intuitively knew that being vulnerable and asking for help was not a weakness but a strength that allowed me to do better and break the cycle.

Three months after the wedding, the young woman found out she was pregnant. Her husband knew what she had been through and that she would never tolerate abuse to her or her children. This man she had chosen was loving and gentle, and she was wrapped up in love with her new life.

On June 28, 1957, I was born, and it didn't take long for the chaos to start.

At a year old, I started having bladder infections that, by age four, damaged my right kidney. I was screaming inconsolably, and the doctor told Mom to get me to emergency immediately. I had a six-hour operation that would hopefully make it all better. It didn't, and I continued to be hospitalized regularly with temperatures of up to 106°F. Mom was so stressed being up with me in the night checking my temperature, not to mention the regular trips she had to make with me to the doctor and to emergency, while Dad slept because he had to work the next day.

I have always loved my mom. Although she was unpredictable, she was fiercely protective of her family and loved Dad and me more than life itself. That being said, when I was alone with her, I never knew when her mood would turn, so I worked at being on my best behaviour so as not to get her angry.

Often when she yelled and said hurtful things, I would run to my bedroom. She would come in behind me, crying, telling me how sorry she was and that she didn't mean what she said. I knew she loved me, but it was so confusing.

Running parallel to this single-minded mission of keeping me well and running the household as a stay-at-home mom, Mom encountered the same feelings she had experienced as a youngster growing up—anxiety, anger, and lack of control, which manifested as rage. The only ones around to take it out on were Dad and me. Verbal and emotional abuse was common, and her moods were unpredictable.

With a strong need to control, Mom used perfecting as her way to hide the shame, fear, and anxiety she couldn't escape. Unfortunately, when she numbed the negative by trying to control, she also numbed the positive emotions such as joy, gratitude, and happiness. This woman had perfected the art of perfecting, but it was not pretty.

I vividly recall being about seven years old and shopping for back-to-school clothes. Looking back at photos now, I see a beautiful little girl, but when I came out of that dressing room, nothing I tried on was acceptable. Mom started yelling, "Nothing fits you properly, I can't put you in any of the pretty dresses other girls wear. We'll have to find a tent dress."

As Mom was yelling, numerous people moved away, while Dad tried softly talking to her to calm her down. But no one ever stood up to her or came to my defense; Mom seemed all-powerful.

I stood there crying, feeling full of shame. Why couldn't I just be perfect like other girls? Why did I have to always make her so mad?

Another time, Mom stayed in bed while I got ready for school. When she got up, I wasn't as far along as she would have liked. Considering I was only about eight years old, I think I could have been forgiven for getting waylaid.

She was so mad that she lifted me up on the kitchen counter so her face was right in mine. With a butter knife in her hand, she was yelling and screaming in my face, looking at me eyeball to eyeball, smashing the knife down on the edge of the counter immediately beside me.

I was terrified for my life and crying uncontrollably saying, "Mommy, please don't hurt me, don't hurt me."

I know now that she was doing everything in her power to keep from hitting me. She was trying her best to control her life, but the pent-up emotions inside had to get out. However, the little girl sitting on the counter learned in that moment that she was a worthless failure.

Often when the rages or dark moods took place, Mom would have a bath or go to bed early to have time by herself. In hindsight, I can see that she never really had an outlet while I was sick. She was afraid to travel, so vacations were out, and the few we took were stressful. I lived vicariously through my friends when they went on vacation and loved getting their postcards from afar.

Around twelve years of age, my health stabilized, and Mom could finally let her foot off the pedal. Except she couldn't. She had been on high alert for so long that she had a delayed aftershock, what we might now consider PTSD. She was briefly hospitalized while they did tests; the immense stress she had taken on throughout her life had caught up to her.

As I started high school, Mom relaxed some and was easier to be around, giving me room to grow and learn to be independent and responsible. However, her perfectionism was now rubbing off on me. Although I was popular at school, I had very low self-esteem and self-worth, a secret I grappled with much of my life. I couldn't seem to unite who I was outwardly with my inner critic.

In the midst of everything, Dad was a calm stabilizing influence in our household who could roll with Mom's moods that were still a part of our lives. I noticed his quiet strength, love, and patience, but it took years to understand how much he offered. We were blessed to have Dad in our lives.

After high school, I worked at a drug store and then passionately pursued a career as a sales representative. I was successful and loved what I did; however, with each promotion, I felt unworthy, like I did not fit despite the fact I continually overachieved.

As an adult, I had always tried to get Mom and Dad out by taking them to dinner, live theatre, and the ballet. Occasionally, they even joined me and my girlfriends at nightclubs. They had met dancing back in the '50s, so it was great to see them having fun now. I even got Mom to take the gondola up Grouse Mountain for lunch one Mother's Day. I liked doing things where I was taking control, showing Mom I was capable.

One day a few years later when I was visiting them, Mom said, "It's too bad we never really did the things that mothers and daughters do." She was obviously reflecting back on her life with her mom. Grandma lived downtown and they would always meet and bum around, checking store deals, and having lunch together. To my mom, that was what mothers and daughters did. It broke my heart that she could not see a new tradition in the many wonderful things we did together.

In 1988, I met my future husband at a work function. He was handsome, charming, and fun, with a big personality. Unfortunately, Mom saw Ken as a threat.

We got married in 1992 and moved to Calgary, Alberta, and I was grateful to also gain an amazing son just fifteen years my junior. This, however, was more reason for Mom to feel resentment.

My mom was angry that I had allowed Ken to take me away, and it was me who had to go visit her regularly because she was afraid to travel. When I visited her, I stayed in her home, and everything was on her terms. I could not even meet with a friend for coffee.

Now I am reminded of the saying, "We teach people how to treat us."

I was successfully navigating the emotional landmines via phone, but while visiting Mom, it was taking a toll on me. Emotionally exhausted, I asked the universe for help because I was not happy with how I was being treated. I was so thirsty for knowledge on how to live life on my terms.

Mom believed everything was her way or the wrong way, and I was beginning to learn specific strategies to deal with her. As I learned to take back my power and be responsible for my thoughts, feelings, and actions, I was better able to control my happiness. It was not about others changing, it was all about feeding my inner critic new information and overcoming beliefs that were holding me back. I realized if I was to keep moving forward, I needed to continue finding worth in myself, which meant never giving up.

I thank the many teachers who came into my life and imparted their knowledge, as well as the great books I devoured, such as *The Seat of the Soul* by Gary Zukav and everything Brené Brown teaches. I did not just pay lip service to the lessons, I worked to implement the processes and actively integrate what I had learned. This was the most important work I have ever done. Ken saw the changes in me and wanted to learn and grow as well. Thankfully, we now have a strong, equal relationship based on mutual respect.

In 2014, after twenty-four years in Calgary, Ken and I moved back to British Columbia to a city two hours away from Mom. Ken's parents and my dad had died years earlier, and with Mom now in her mid-eighties, this would bring us closer to her. Her three-bedroom townhouse with lots of stairs, far from shopping is now getting to her, but she refuses to move. She is upset that her only child has *still* abandoned her, but I know I am close enough to be there when needed—if she'd only allow me or anyone to assist. She will always give, but she cannot allow herself to receive, which is a hurtful imbalance. It's hurtful for the giver to never have an open heart to receive, as well as for the receiver, who builds up resentment at the imbalance of power.

Over the years, I have learned that the only person I control is me. I have worked long and hard through my challenges. Unfortunately, Mom has built a wall to stay safe and it is just too thick to penetrate. Although I am sad for the person she could have been if she had gotten help, I have compassion for the painful journey she has had. Unfortunately, compassion does not make it any easier. On one hand, she laments that everyone has abandoned her, while on the other, she pushes everyone away, including me.

All the work I have done has allowed me to honour my mom and be there for her as best as I can, even when she pushes me away. While this can be painful, it has also allowed me to accept the lopsided reality of our relationship.

Although it has been a progression over decades, I am finally integrating all that I have learned. I am now living a more passionate and meaningful life and am committed to sharing my journey. As Brené Brown says in her books *Daring Greatly* and *Rising Strong*, "Vulnerability is not weakness, it is courage." I have been courageous all of my life, and it has made all the difference.

In the Darkest Hours
by Brenda Hammon

I was fifteen and had been under a huge amount of stress due to the sexual and mental abuse I'd experienced since the age of five. I didn't care if I lived or died, my life had no meaning, and according to my abusers, I was disposable. I believed them.

I had lived for ten years without a care for my own wellbeing or safety. I did crazy things like swim in the nearby river that had claimed the lives of many people who actually could swim. No one asked where I went all day, and I didn't tell. It was safer for me than staying on the farm where our family lived.

One night in bed, I was awakened by a strange sensation. I didn't move, but just opened my eyes and watched a knife blade in the pitch darkness hovering beside me. I could see the moonlight flicker off the blade as it started to move backward and forward. Most people would have screamed, but not me. I just lay there waiting for the blade to slash and stab me. I hoped that with my death I would finally be free of all the pain I had been holding. So, I simply closed my eyes, breathed a sigh of release, and waited for the end. When I awoke the next morning, I was deeply disappointed to realize that I was, indeed, still alive, still in pain, still profoundly sad that I had to live this life of disappointments from those that were supposed to love, protect, and guide me.

I am forty-four years old, and I am lying in my childhood bedroom again, thinking how strange it is to be back here again after all this time.

All is quiet in the house, and darkness has come. I know I should be asleep, but for some reason, sleep is avoiding me this night. My mind has been in such a turmoil for the past few days, with Alfred's sudden death and the anger and vile energy from his parents and siblings toward me. I never thought that they would outright blame me for his death.

Alfred's family and my oldest brother had arranged a special meeting involving me, and earlier today, I'd found myself being pressured into this meeting on the pretense that it would help my daughters deal with their father's death. Within minutes of entering Alfred's parents' house, I was hit with this heavy negative energy, and I found it hard to breath. I felt like someone was choking me, trying to end my life.

I managed to sit down at the kitchen table across from his mother and father. Alfred's mother could barely contain her hatred for me and blurted out that it was my fault that her son was dead.

Shocked at her outburst, I looked from her to his father, who seemed to have aged twenty years in the last week. I pushed myself up from the table and looked at the rest of his family, then back at his disgusting mother sitting there with contempt, glaring at me. I simply stated, "I didn't kill your son; he did that on his own." With that, I managed to get out the door and into my waiting vehicle to leave that place of hell behind me.

Now tonight lying in bed, sleep finally comes.

But suddenly in the quiet of the still dark night, I'm awake again as I feel a presence in the room. I instantly know who it is. I can't see him, but I know deep down in my soul that it is Alfred standing in the corner watching me. He has followed me from his parents place to here. Why is he here? Is it because in three more days I will be attending his funeral? Does he think I am here for him, or does he know I am only here in support of our daughters?

Strangely, I don't feel afraid of him now that he is dead. It feels ironic really, for he had created such hatred toward me after the separation, and for these past three years with the divorce, that I feared him. While he was alive, I knew that if he had the chance, he would kill me or keep me captive somehow. I knew that he thought that if he could not have me at his disposal then nobody would. I knew deep down in my soul that this world was not big enough for the two of us to survive such hatred and possessiveness. After his death, I guess I am still in the belief that a dead man can't hurt you. I will soon learn the folly in that belief.

Within a week after the funeral, things start to happen in Bud's and my home. Little things that at first, I excuse as coincidence. A feeling of being watched, goose bumps on my arms. Even when my bed suddenly shakes in the middle of night, I try to reason it away. Maybe I am dreaming; maybe it's hormones.

This all changes when I finally see Alfred standing at the foot of my bed with a sneer on his face. My first thought is, "Oh shit, he's finally found me." I believe he followed me home after his funeral. After three years of hiding from him in life, a sickening feeling comes over me. Nighttime will never be, for me, a time to relax and sleep peacefully. That possibility is shattered. I have no idea what to do. I just hope that he will eventually go away.

I had been foolish to believe that when a person dies they go away to heaven or hell; I soon realize that this is not the case. Alfred is once more tormenting me, but this time I cannot hide from him. There's no place that I can go to escape his wrath; now he has full access to me from the other side.

The occurrences of his arrival every night have been happening for three months now, and I never told Bud what was going on. I didn't want him to think that I was crazy, even though he had stood by me through all the crap that Alfred had dished out while he was alive.

Both Bud and I are awakened in the middle of one night by a loud crash in our walk-in closet. I'm terrified to get up and go open that closet door, so I nudge Bud and asked him if he also heard the crash in the closet. Surprisingly, Bud had heard it, too.

Bud slips out of bed, walks across the room to the closet, and opens the door, fully expecting to be greeted with all our clothes laying on the floor. But everything is as it was, nothing out of place. A cold chill runs down my back bone and the hairs on the back of my neck and arms stand at attention. I know deep down in the pit of my stomach that Alfred is not going to go away any time soon. He's having too much fun, and my fear of him is ramping up. In that moment, despair and defeat become my friend.

The straw that breaks the camel's back comes on New Year's Eve when Bud and I are cuddling by the fireplace on the carpet. I have my eyes closed as Bud snuggles into my neck. When I open my eyes and look at Bud, Alfred is staring back. It's Alfred's face and his eyes. I quickly shut my eyes, and when I reopen them, Bud is staring at me. Relief washes over me. I don't tell Bud what happened, but it sure is a mood killer for me.

I can't figure out what to do. I feel that I'm going crazy. I've been refusing to understand or accept what has been happening to me. My mind just couldn't go there, into the darkness where Alfred now resided. But, try as I might, I also can't ignore these occurrences anymore. Within a week, I make an appointment with my new doctor, Dr. Brooks. I don't know if she will think that I'm crazy or if this is really real. I don't even know. Am I being haunted, or is this my imagination created by all the stress I'm under? I need answers.

Dr. Brooks advises that I should go and see one of her colleagues who deals with grief, so off I go to meet Lorraine. I'm hoping that this will be a simple process, but I have a rude awakening with the answer that I receive from Lorraine.

Lorraine tells me that I have to get control of and deal with Alfred and his constant haunting of me. This is both life altering and downright scary. I am not prepared for what I will have to do to rid myself of my dead ex-husband and retain my sanity. If I ever thought that what I had gone through so far in my life was bad, well this is going to be epic on a whole new, unfamiliar level.

For the next several months, I have to learn how to block Alfred and his attacks. Most times, I feel that I'm at a loss as to how to gain my power back. The more I try to block him, the stronger he becomes.

The simple technique of putting up a barrier, thinking and envisioning my invisible wall, was not working. I had to figure out something else, but what?

At times, I feel like I'm fighting the devil himself; his anger and hatred are sickening and terrifying. Lorraine tells me I need an energy tool kit, but I have no tools to handle an aggressive spirit and, trying to wrap my head around all the things that he had gained power in doing is disturbing, to say the least. For instance, Alfred makes sure that he's with me during every visit to see Lorraine. He stands in the corner with his arms crossed over his chest, listening and smirking.

During one of my visits to Lorraine, Alfred jumps into my body. While I'm struggling to get him out, his mother suddenly jumps in too. Now both are fighting inside to see who's going to be the first to channel through me. My body feels like it is being ripped apart from the inside out. I'm having a hard time breathing, and my whole insides are trembling under the weight of the negative energy coursing through my body. It takes several hours before we are able to evacuate them, and I'm drained by the process. Fear has been firmly planted into my soul, for if I had any doubts in my limited ability to deal with Alfred, they are confirmed this day. I feel that he is way too powerful for me to handle on my own. Also, I am determined to never let him into my body again, even though I have no idea how he got in in the first place.

Lorraine tells me to go home and ask for help to stop Alfred from entering my body again, so I do. I'm unsure who to ask, so I just pray that night for someone to tell me what to do.

The following day, I call Lorraine and tell her that I had a vision of wearing an amulet. I tell her that it had to be in the shape of a human heart, made out of mammoth tusk. I think to myself, this is so stupid, where I am going to find mammoth tusk? For heaven's sake, they are extinct and have been for a very long time. Again, I am at a loss, but within a few days, Lorraine calls with the name of a man who can help me.

Soon, I start wearing a heart amulet. Then later, I wear stones and crystals to absorb Alfred's negative energy. Finally, I wear the Saint Christopher necklace that Bud had bought me when we first got together. I am determined not to let Alfred near me, and in doing so, I start to shut down my spiritual gift (or curse) of feeling him around me. Spiritually, I don't know how to ask for help from my guides or the archangels. This is all foreign to me, so I soldier on, trying to deflect him as best as I can.

As the years roll by, I continued to be in defense mode, and soon my heart and energy are completely closed off. I am encased in a solid cocoon, feeling nothing. This is the only way I feel I can survive this life on earth.

At the beautiful age of fifty-seven years old, Hughie enters my life. Hughie is a 17.2 hh chestnut Warmblood gelding that I've purchased as my next riding horse. Hughie has been in my life for only two weeks, and I worry he's depressed because he's left his home. A friend of mine asks an animal whisperer named Mary to come to talk to Hughie, to let him know that I am his new owner. I'm not too sure about this animal whispering thing, but I'm willing to give it a try for Hughie's sake.

All is going okay, and Mary is telling Hughie that he's going to enjoy his new home and his new owner, but Hughie does not understand. Instead, he communicates his concern about me to Mary. Apparently, he can't see my heart or feel my energy. This bothers him, and he tells Mary that he can't bond with me unless he can see my heart and feel me.

When Mary turns to me and tells me what Hughie felt, cold air washes over my body. I stand there looking at this big, beautiful soul of a horse, and tears brim my eyes in the realization that he's right. For the past ten years, I have allowed Alfred to hurt me on a soul level, and now is the time to put a stop to all of that. So that I can connect with Hughie and with other people who want to be in my life, I have to face my fears.

Hughie becomes the catalyst for me to finally figure out what basic positive tools I need in my energy tool kit, like accepting help from others, to trust with my heart again and not just with my mind, and to forgive myself. Those were some pretty big positive tools in that little tool box. I also realized that I had to relearn how to accept love without allowing the negative to slide right in and take over. I have to conquer my own fear, and I'm not sure if I can trust myself again to be open and accepting after over forty-five years of hiding the real me.

I find out that Mary also does energetic work with people, and I ask for her help. The following week, Mary arrives at our house to help me do a clearing on myself, but what happens is something out of a horror movie.

Mary does a walkthrough of our house and says that she has to clear our house, and not me. She says that she can feel the negative energy in our den and that is where she will start. We aren't sure how long it's going to take for her to deal with what is there, so Bud and I wait in the living room for Mary to emerge. After a few hours, we both wanted to see what was going on, but Mary had instructed us not to disturb her, so we waited. The house was so quiet, like a tomb, while we waited and waited and waited. Neither one of us was interested in going outside to putter around, we both were nervous and excited at the same time but also scared as to what she was finding and dealing with.

After four hours, we start to get worried and think, "Holy crap, has she died in there?" But finally, Mary emerges from the den with a pile of note papers in her hand. Both Bud and I wait for the verdict about what had transpired. We are shocked. As we sit there listening to Mary give her report, another wave of despair rolls over me. To find out that Alfred and his deceased, miserable mother, Wheezy, were residing in the den causing chaos for Bud, me, and my daughters was numbing. Wheezy was also attacking the horses because she knew how she could hurt me, while Alfred was affecting Bud's blood pressure by spiking it. Thankfully, Bud was a pretty grounded guy, and with high blood pressure in his family, he attributed his increase to family genetics. Alfred could not attack me as I was so closed off, so instead, he attacked our daughters knowing that that would affect me emotionally and mentally. When Mary finally finished her report, I didn't think that I can handle much more.

Over the next four years, it becomes a battle of the wills—Alfred vs Brenda—and it's a knockdown, drag 'em out fight for my survival and existence in the living world. Some battles I win and some I lose, but all I know is that I have to win the war. I have to finally be free from him and his torment, to be able to live my life on my terms, without fear of him and the unknown. To be able to be spiritual and to maybe one day explore the empathic and intuitive gifts that I have. To feel that I can be open to others and to feel full love without fear. To finally be the real me, whoever that may be, for I have no idea.

I try all forms of therapy to help rid myself of Alfred and my past, and during these sessions, Alfred roars forward to show his dominance over me. Then, three years after Mary cleared our house, Thyra enters my life.

On my first visit with her for cellular release from my past sexual abuse as a child, Alfred does his usual thing and roars right in, trying to take over.

He calls Thyra a lot of horrible names and tells her to leave, that I belong to him, and for her to "F off." I sit quietly through it all, as I can tell by her body and the look on her face she knows what is happening.

Thyra looks at me while Alfred is screaming his venom at her and asks me to wait a minute while she deals with this negative energy. Sitting there watching Thyra with her eyes closed, taking deep, slow breaths to keeping her grounded, I am curious to see how this was going to play out. I wonder if she is spiritually strong enough to deal with his maliciousness. I didn't have to wait long for that answer. When she's done, she explains to me that she's sealed Alfred in a clear energetic cylinder with an opening at the top and bottom so that he's free to go up to the light or down to wherever that would take him, his choice. But now he can no longer affect me.

Alfred chooses neither and stays in the cylinder, watching, screaming, and having tantrums at times, but through it all, he can't reach me anymore with his harmful energy.

With all the help from Thyra and others, I finally realize that I am a very strong empath, and with this, I gain my own power.

Since then, for the last several years, I have no longer been afraid of my past or of Alfred. I have been freed to look into what spiritual gifts I have and to slowly expand on my abilities.

I was so afraid to explore this part of me and had shut it down because that was how I thought I needed to survive, but now having gained my own power, fear is no longer my constant companion. I have realized that my gifts are unique to me and that I don't have to do it the same way as another person. Each medium or empath that has come into my life has taught me another level of me, and now I am free to truly be me and to embrace my own unique gifts. Every day, I surprise myself with my abilities, and I try to remain open to all of it while at the same time knowing that I can close the door and take a break from all the psychic energy that flows around me.

Now, I have to thank Alfred for all of his attempts to destroy me, as I have become the victor. I have learned so many things because of him that I would not have learned otherwise. I have learned that I am strong, determined, and not a pushover. I have value, I am an empath with many gifts, I am loved for being me, and I am one hell of a woman who deserves everything she asks for in life. I am no longer hindered in seeking what I want in life. I am no longer afraid of things that go bump in the night, for now I know that I have the wisdom and courage to tackle what comes my way. I am now able to help departed souls find their own way home if they are lost, for I am a beacon of light that shines bright for all those that choose to see through the thin veil that separates us all in this life and the next.

It took a long time, but I have finally found out who I am through the darkest hours.

Finding Freedom
by Jeanine LeBlanc

B abies need something to cry about," Dad said. "I will give you a reason to cry."

I was seven years old, locked in my bedroom for being a child. I remember looking out into the distant calm from my bedroom window. This is where I watched an old, abandoned farmhouse far off in a lightly treed field. The structure stood silent and mysterious. As a young child, I was a tomboy who loved to venture out into the deep woods. Some days I chose the path not taken, and other days there was no path at all.

The day came when my best friend, my brother, and I skipped down our street through the private military quarters in the direction of the farmhouse. The three of us played through a side street then continued into the brush until we met up with some train tracks. I remember the rocks between the tracks were black with beautiful specks of blue, yellow, and red. I danced along, picking up a hand full at a time. With pockets full of gems, we soon began to settle down for our lunch.

While unfolding our picnic blanket, we were startled by a couple of teenage boys walking down the tracks. I recognized one of the boys as a nearby neighbor. The other I had never seen before. We ate our sandwiches, and the boys talked for a while before the familiar teenager said his farewells.

Afterward, the stranger disappeared into the nearby brush. As an intuitive child, I began to grow uneasy with our new strange friend. My gut wrenched when he returned from the brush claiming he lost his pocketknife and wanted my brother's assistance to locate it. Feeling desperate, I went over and peered through the brush to find this young man sitting on a stump. My brother stood between his legs with his pants and underwear pulled down. Immediately, I screamed for him to let my little brother go. I hurled my beautiful rocks though the bushes until the stranger ran into view and further down the railroad tracks. I later found out the stranger never lost his knife at all. He had it held against my brother's penis. Needless to say, our journey to the farmhouse had ended.

After joining our quivering hands, we ran and cried the entire way home. Once we arrived at our house, my friend carried on down the street to her family. My brother and I tiredly ran inside our house, exhausted. We stood there in the hallway sobbing uncontrollably and barely able to catch our breath. As frightened, vulnerable children, we needed our parents' love and safety.

Unfortunately, our house delivered the opposite.

I will never forget my little brother and I standing in the hallway trying to tell my father why we were crying, but we just couldn't get the words out. No words. My father grew anxious and decided he would give us a "real" reason to cry. We stood in the hallway up against the wall while my father slapped and kicked us both repeatedly. We cried for the fear, pain, vulnerability, and disbelief.

Once we were finally heard by our parents, the military police drove over for our statements. My brother and I separately looked through numerous pictures of teenage boys to assist in the identification. My little being sat there feeling trapped. It was this day that I can recall learning that I needed to be the strongest I could ever be, for me, my brother, and sister.

My mother was both exceptional and scary. I loved and feared her. She was extremely smart, outgoing, and talented with her artwork. I remember her loving arms when she held me on her lap. But I also recall her ripping hair from my head with the brush while I sat between her knees.

Through childhood, our mother introduced my sister, brother, and me to multiple forms of punishment from being locked up, tied up, and humiliated without clothing and lined up for bare belt whippings. Being third in line to get bare whipped by a belt was terrifying. For the tears on my siblings' cheeks and the horror in their eyes, I have never felt so much compassion and fear at once.

I was eleven years old when our mom drowned at a public beach while trying to save a young girl's life. She was swept beneath the dark ocean waters by a whirling undertow. The young girl survived, leaving my mother the hero I always knew she could be. Our childhood years to come remained abusive. I held my strength and dried the tears I knew as a little girl. We cried out with our fists in the air to shield our bodies from the blows and to show our father that we still loved ourselves.

After quitting school at seventeen years old, I enlisted in the Canadian armed forces as an army cook. Here, I felt right at home with new forms of discipline and the familiar feeling of being trapped. I also found myself attracted to certain women. I found a passion I had not known until the first time I kissed the soft lips of another woman. I began to date the person I liked; "proper" gender was no longer a necessity. After two years in the forces, I experienced both emotional and sexual abuse for my attraction to women. I was mistreated and abused in the very kitchen I cooked in. After applying for my release from the forces after only two years, I desperately waited for the reply of my release date. Life, however, hadn't handed me the tools I needed to make it through my turmoil. Without support, I soon found myself AWOL. I was lost. But even though I felt lost, I felt found. I was finally free.

Only weeks later, I fearfully turned myself into military headquarters. During my court martial, the superior officer informed me of his awareness of my sexual harassment. He said that if I gave the names of those who sexually harassed and abused me, I would not be sent to the Canadian military prison. I chose to take my secret to prison with me. Had I known the severity of military prison, I may have chosen differently. Now I was trapped and punished, all my sentenced twenty-one days long. I was forced to say nothing to anyone. I could not cry tears. Preceding my time in prison, I returned to the kitchen to work alongside those I kept hidden within my secret.

Following the military, I worked for several delivery companies and eventually learned all aspects of the business. At twenty-five years old, I was confident and determined to succeed at my own business. I tiredly worked at building my company through the day and drove cash deliveries by night as my customer list grew. After a few years, my company contracted nineteen drivers, employed three office staff, and billed out nearly $1 million annually. During my time of success, truth be told, I also contracted a near-fatal love for illegal drugs.

On a September day, just a year into growing my company, I stood in my office and played my morning messages. "Your dad died of a heart attack last night," was what I thought I had heard in the voice of my father's companion. In disbelief, I replayed the message over again. And again.

Nothing would ever feel the same as a mid-twenties orphan. My rusted anchor detached, and I sailed through life like a ghost at sea. My soul danced while clenching the intensities of gambling, alcohol, cocaine, crack cocaine, and, sometimes, meth. I could not cry genuine tears for my father's sudden passing. Instead, I found an emptiness deeper than the barren pockets of where I once held the colorful rocks of the railroad. I moved into the unknown where I flirted with the dark dimensions between living and dying.

My ultimate days and nights consisted of blackjack tables, vodka paralyzers, and lines of cocaine through the doors of a casino washroom. There would generally be a girlfriend or another "friend" around to make the money disco more attractive and seductive. Ultimately, I was playing into everything deadly in order to feel at all alive.

Then, eventually, I did die inside. I died after losing my home and all of the money made from selling my delivery business. I stopped loving all things and wrapped my soul in shame and pain. I left my friend's couch and drove aimlessly in my car with my two cats and a few belongings. After a phone call to my New York family, sister, and best friend, I called my dear friend in Edmonton. She said she had a room for me and wanted me to stay at her home so I could work at getting my life back together.

In Edmonton, I quickly found a pulse, and my light began to shine. Only a month after quitting drugs, I joined roller derby, and for many years to come, I worked hard to be an athlete. I also trained and became a Canadian certified boxer. My soul poured out like a fountain of strength from the great beyond. To love myself, I needed to exhilarate within the power of rawness and realness.

During this time, I also found employment in traffic law enforcement as a peace officer and worked alongside the Edmonton city police. I became a sergeant, a trainer, and ran a crew of officers. Nothing had felt more surreal than to have once ran from the law and later to become a leader within. Being followed into work by police vehicles some days felt kind of freaky until reminding myself of the realities.

After a couple years at my new job, one day during a Reiki session, my mother came to me through a meditation. I asked her why she left her children so young, and she replied, "Because I love you." I powerfully understood the path I had been walking and that I needed to travel alone to become the strong and loving woman I am. Every fall became uplifting as the shame and blame rolled away. I also began to share the story of the last time I had ever seen my father. Early on in the year of his heart attack, my father traveled six hundred kilometers from where he lived in Saskatoon. He drove to Calgary only to see me. On route, he broke down but continued by Greyhound bus. It was this time my father shared a reason to cry. He wept as he apologized for how he abused us as children and expressed how proud he was for each of us. Through my parents' deaths, I later learned how we were once truly loved, so imperfectly.

Today, at forty-five years old, I live happily here on Nova Scotia's eastern shore. My acreage is home to nearly thirty rescued animals with needs. I built another business to afford the cost of loving them.

Like a farmer, while the stars dance across the night sky, I rise to feed and care for my sweet and wild friends. And before each morning sunrise, I play a few familiar songs and dance amongst their energy between the loving walls of our country home. I dance for their happiness...I dance like a fool for my free and beautiful now.

You Are Never Too Old to Start a New Venture
by Sue Ferreira

Curled up in the fetal position on the bed, I felt nothing.

I had been there unmoving for hours, after realizing my marriage of thirty-seven years was over. I wasn't able to think or make decisions about "what's next?" I felt as dead as you could be, while still being alive.

Suddenly, from nowhere, I felt a warm glow suffusing my body. I felt as though I had been given a shot of morphine.

What happened remains a mystery to this day, but my body was being reawakened by a flood of endorphins, which gave me the strength and resolve to get up off the bed, leave my marriage, and face my new life with confidence and a certainty that my new path would be fulfilling and successful.

For over thirty years, I had practiced medicine as an anesthesiologist. I know the comfort and relief morphine can bring to a soul, and I know about endorphins.

Where and why they flooded my body at this time, I will never know.

Why this awakening came at that moment and where it came from will remain a mystery, but my reanimation and that transformational moment will stay with me forever.

This was August 2007, and at age sixty, I set off into my new life of a single woman heading into her later years.

Here's the rub—over my decades in medicine, I have witnessed our increasing longevity, especially the long lives many women are living. I've watched the growing numbers of independently living, fit, and spry women in their mid-nineties appearing in the operating room for new knees and hips, and I've seen them leave to continue to live their fulfilling lives.

Although it looks like we will all be living longer, few of us are emotionally and financially prepared for living to well beyond a hundred. Given that by age one hundred, women outnumber men five to one, women need to be prepared for the likelihood that they may be alone in their later years.

In my first year of being alone, I realized I needed to learn how to manage my money, so I began reading everything I could lay my hands on about money and finances. This was now 2008, and the more I read, the more I became concerned about the machinations of the financial world, which came to a head with the financial crisis.

A couple of weeks after the crash, I was standing in the operating room lunch room, waiting for my next patient, and watching the US congress reject the bill that was supposed to reboot the economy.

I knew this rejection would crash the stock markets the next day and that millions of innocent people would lose their hard-earned savings, investments, homes, and livelihoods. At first, I was angry—very angry at the arrogance, hubris, corruption, and incompetence of the financial and political worlds.

Suddenly, my anger became nausea, as in my mind, I saw myself standing on the edge of a cliff, looking down into a massive valley filled with the people who were about to lose everything. I felt weak at the knees thinking about the challenges they would face in the coming decade. Many in my age group, heading into their later years, would not have the time to recover their losses and would struggle in the coming years.

Then, from out of nowhere, a little voice said to me, "Someone needs to do something to help these people recover from this hit."

Another voice said, "Well, you are 'Someone,' why don't you help them? You've put your life back on track."

"Not in a million years," I replied.

A call that my next patient arrived brought me back to the real world, but the vision of those people who were about to lose so much would not go away. Later that evening, I said to myself, "Well, maybe I can help them in some way."

Enter my second turning point, the follow up to that moment when I was flooded with endorphins and found the courage to leave my marriage. This second turning point would take me in a new and unexpected direction, leading me to helping women make that extra money they would need to see them through their later years and to writing this story today.

A decade later, my awareness that many would realize they will run out of money before they run out of life is now evident, as many women aged fifty-five and older set out on the journey of building a business later in life.

Deciding to help others generate income for their later years was the easy step. How to accomplish this was different ball game! I had never run a business. I had never had to seek out clients. Health care has a never-ending stream of patients. You never have to search for them. I knew I wanted to help people recover from the hit of 2008, but I wasn't sure how. Some part of me suspected technology would be involved.

Since 1984, when we bought our first computer, I knew the Internet would become a powerful force in our lives, yet even in 2008, the web did not have the hold on our lives it does today.

It's difficult to imagine today, but in 2008, the iPhone was brand new. Facebook and YouTube were in their infancy, and there were no educational programs of the sophistication of today. Still, I knew then that to be successful in a new venture, any start-up entrepreneur would need to understand and use the web to grow their business. Yet, I saw these web skills were sorely lacking amongst those in their later years, who grew up without the web and who felt it was all new-fangled nonsense.

Even today, these web skills are lacking for many women over fifty-five, the largest demographic starting new businesses. They need their new businesses to be successful, but without web skills, they will not be able to compete in today's digital world, but it is precisely this demographic who have the wisdom needed by so many across the world.

By our fifties, we have all been knocked about a bit and learned a thing or two about life. Our wisdom is valuable and needed, but how do we take that wisdom out into the world?

The under-thirties have the web tech know-how, but limited life experience. The over-fifties have the life experience, but not the tech know-how. Web tech has simplified significantly and now can be learned easily. Now in my seventies, I knew that if I could do this, others could too, and I could show them how.

My first attempt at building an online business was a bust. I presumed that anyone heading into their later years would be interested in making some added income, so they could Live Their Retirement Dream—the name of my first business.

How wrong could I be?

I was still a novice at marketing and business, but I quickly realized that few were interested in doing anything in their retirement. After all, they were retired, but we are living in rapidly changing times. Retirement is an endangered event, and, in truth, many will never retire.

Joining women's networking groups, I realized many women entrepreneurs and business owners were struggling to understand and use the new technologies of the web. They knew they needed to have a bigger web presence and that being visible was key to their success, but they didn't know how to be found, seen, and heard.

I had found my tribe. I changed my focus to women entrepreneurs and business owners and created Wisdom To Wealth Mastery, where I show women how to take their wisdom to a wide audience, to the world, with video.

While building Live Your Retirement Dream, I'd become aware of the rapid rise and power of video in marketing. The perfect storm of YouTube, Facebook, and the smartphone have revolutionized our ability to be seen and heard. Today, it is difficult for any business to succeed without using video.

The whippersnappers of thirty and younger are completely at home with video, but for women over forty-five, being seen and heard on video is a much greater challenge. We grew up in a world where we were conditioned to be invisible. Children should be seen and not heard was the message of my childhood.

Changing your mindset and developing the confidence to be seen and heard takes courage. More times than I can remember, I have heard, "I can't make a video today, my hair's not right," or "I need to lose ten pounds before I make any videos," when the true message is "I am not comfortable being seen by the world."

With Wisdom To Wealth Mastery, I love seeing women's faces light up when I show them video is fun and they realize they can help more people by taking their message far and wide, while also making added income.

I was on a roll, but life was about to send me another curve ball, teaching me yet another lesson.

In the summer of 2017, with Wisdom To Wealth Mastery growing well, I knew there was something going on in my left breast. I had some early signs of breast cancer, and by pure serendipity, my routine mammogram appointment arrived in the mail, which I took this as a sign to get moving.

As expected, my mammogram and biopsy were positive, so I had a mastectomy in the fall of 2017. I am one of the lucky ones who caught their cancer early before it spread, so a mastectomy was all I required.

What was the life lesson from this curve ball? It's one I saw every day of my life when I was an anesthesiologist—"shit happens," and life can change in a second.

Almost every day, in the operating room, my coworkers and I saw, with sadness, a patient whose life and the lives of his or her family members had changed, possibly forever. And now, my life had changed.

I was able to keep Wisdom To Wealth Mastery ticking over the seven months between my diagnosis and final surgery, but my mind was not fully present. I lost momentum, and rebuilding momentum has taken some time.

My last surgery was four months ago, at the time of writing. I am up and running again, but it has taken months to rebuild my contacts and visibility.

I have been blessed in so many ways. Now, in my seventies, with new medical technologies, I know I may have another fifty years of good-quality life ahead of me, so I am preparing for this possibility.

Remember the old Chinese proverb, "May you live in interesting times"? We are living in interesting times. We are privileged to be living in what I see as the most exciting time in all of human history, a time of unparalleled opportunity. n this golden age of growth and discovery, we have been gifted with the ability to travel our own voyage of discovery.

All it takes is curiosity, a willingness to learn and change, and an openness to those transformational moments and turning points.

I love that every day I find, connect, and help inspiring people I would never have been able to reach a decade ago.

I love that every day, I wake up wondering, whom will I meet today? Who will I help reach their dreams today?

I cannot imagine a better life than this.

They Call Me "Angel"
by Susan Janzen

For years, I felt alone in my deep sadness of never knowing my father or any father figure. Constant questions went unanswered. Who is my father? What was he like? Does he know about me? Is he still alive? That dark, empty hole is something I felt since I was a very young child, and it has affected me tremendously. However, determination stirred in me that day, on my thirteenth birthday, when my mother sat me down and showed me a photo and told me about my father. Since then, I have had a greater self-awareness and a purpose: to change my life circumstances and to find my father. My lifelong search ended on November 25, 2017.

Today, I am at peace. This is my miracle.

I was an only child, born out of wedlock, and spent most of my childhood scared and anxious because there was no sense of security in my life. To be abandoned as a child, regardless of the circumstances, leaves scars and feelings of unworthiness that cannot easily be erased. These deep-seated feelings resulted from being neglected, abandoned, and abused by my mother who, herself, suffered an even harsher childhood. I was placed in various foster homes, and in one home, when I was five years old, I was repeatedly sexually abused. As soon as I had the courage to tell my mother, she promptly rescued me. I lived with Mom until I was nine and then was placed with two hundred other girls in a convent run by six overwhelmed nuns. Mom was in and out of the hospital for physical and psychological problems, while I spent two-and-a-half long, lonely, and anxious years in the convent, worried about myself and my mother.

Good did come out of living in the convent, however, because that is where I found my safe place. It was in the chapel. A seed was planted in my heart, and I asked to be baptized. My faith started to grow. When I was twelve, my mom brought me home and on my thirteenth birthday, she sat me down, showed me an eight-by-ten photo of a very handsome man, and said, "This is your father. His name is Russell Green. We were in love."

For such an important topic, the conversation was unusually short. Mom told me she loved him very much, but she never told him about me. She gave me a "Happy birthday, one year old" card that was signed "Love Nana Green," and it had a return address from M. Green in Winnipeg. I saw my father's name on the frame of the photo, and my heart leaped. For the first time, I had something I never had before; proof that I had a father and a feeling of hope and determination to find him. That was the day my search began. It was 1969.

It was June, and as soon as I finished grade nine, I moved out on my own. With a wave and a promise that I would finish high school, I hopped on a bus to Calgary. This might have been terrifying for some, but I truly believed that I could take care of myself, just as I always had. I learned a valuable lesson, despite my childhood and the many challenges I faced on my own, and that was that I could count on my heavenly father. I had faith that things would get better and that great things were planned for my future.

I wanted to find my father right away. My search was one never-ending question to every single person I ever met who admitted to being from Winnipeg: "Do you know Russell Green?"

The answer was always, "No."

Over the years, my search involved asking that question, phoning every Green in the Winnipeg phone book, and posting my father's photo on Facebook just in case someone recognized him. Three years ago, I spit into not one, but two tubes—Ancestry.com and 23andMe—and waited patiently for the results. Although my heart was full of hope, I also knew I had to be realistic because my dad would be in his eighties, if he was alive at all.

Through my genome journey, I connected with wonderful people who really understood DNA, but the results were always from my mother's side. I met with one woman who was a second cousin. She was very helpful, and whenever she found a close match she would let me know. It was November 25, 2017, when I received her email that changed my life.

She was excited and told me she found an obituary for Lorne Green who shared a lot of my genomes, and she said that I should check it out. (Just in case you are from the *Bonanza* era, this is not *the* Lorne Green.)

I couldn't believe it. It was the first piece of information I had ever received about my father's family. I remember shaking as I carefully read the obituary, and when I got to the bottom, it said he was predeceased by his sister Jackie and brother Rick Gordon. That did not make sense because my father's name was Russell Green, and I didn't see a Russell anywhere. I read through the names of the surviving relatives and saw Lorne's oldest son's name. I found him on Facebook, took a deep breath, and picked up the phone and called him.

I gently explained who I was and that I had been searching for my father my whole life.

When I told him my dad's name, he said, "Yes. That is my dad's brother. He changed his name to Rick Gordon, but he passed away five years ago. Would you like me to email you his obituary?"

As I hung up the phone, I sat there. I was stunned. Frozen. The tears streamed down my face. Finally, I had proof that my father is dead, after all these years of hoping and praying that he was still alive. The stillness was interrupted when an email popped up on my screen, and I was staring at my dad's obituary. It was surreal. I looked at the photo. Not the face of the young man in the photo I had treasured all these years, but that of an eighty-five-year-old man. I couldn't stop sobbing.

As I sat staring at the screen, a warm feeling of love came over me, and the thought of my mom arose. I realized that it had been exactly ten years to the month since she passed away. I felt her presence as I realized that my search was over. After forty-eight years, it was a miracle. I finally found my father. Sadness enveloped me as I thought of him dying just five years earlier.

But you know that feeling of relief when you lose something precious and then you find it? It is like you can finally, after so long, exhale. I felt so grateful. A sense of peace came over me and was so strong that I realized how differently I felt. My whole life I was always searching, hurrying, rushing, anxious, and I never really understood it until that moment.

The black hole was finally filled with light and that feeling of fear in my gut was gone. As the tears rolled down my cheeks, I realized that my prayers were finally answered, and I had a sense of relief but also feelings of sadness. So many years of wondering if he was dead or alive and visualizing him finding me and hugging me so tight. Now I would never be able to touch him or ask him the questions that had burdened me since I was a little girl.

Then a small voice said to me, "Be still, and know that this is the time when you were meant to find out about your dad; you were not ready until now." I'd heard this voice often in prayer, and I trusted it was right.

Looking back on those years, I was always optimistic about finding my father and never gave up. What is most puzzling to me is that I never gave a thought to the fact that my father may have had other children. Being an only child, I guess it was something that I just never considered.

This is where my story gets exciting. When I finally stopped crying and calmed myself down, I took a closer look at the obituary. I noticed his mother's name was Myrtle, which must be the M. Green I saw on the return address on the happy first birthday card. Then I saw the names of his four surviving children.

What?

He has two sons and two daughters. That means I have four half siblings? If I contacted them, maybe they would tell me about my dad. Exactly how I was going to break this to them, I did not know. My sadness was slowly turning to excitement at the thought of actually speaking to even one of his children. As I brushed the tears from my face, I was hopeful again. Then thoughts kept running through my mind of all the terrible stories I have heard over the years about people reaching out to lost relatives and being rejected or miserable, wishing that they had never tried.

I took a deep breath, looked up their names on Facebook, and found the oldest son, Rick Gordon, Jr. I slowly began typing a private message to him, introducing myself, explaining that I was an only child, and that I had been looking for my dad my whole life. I explained where and when I was born and that I did not want to cause any negative feelings or hurt anyone, I just wanted information about my father. I hoped he would understand. I attached the worn eight-by-ten photo of Dad and clicked "send."

I sat there, so excited but nervous at the same time. I waited. This was the closest I had ever come to finding out about my dad, and I was scared. I wondered if I would get a message saying, "Get lost, you crazy lady."

All of a sudden, I saw the three little bouncing dots on my screen. He was writing me back! I watched the bouncing dots for fifteen of the longest minutes of my life. It felt like an eternity. Will he be nice? What will he say? Will he believe me?

Then a message popped up on my screen! "Hey, Sis...that is a great photo of our dad that I have never seen before. Dad told us about you on his deathbed, but we didn't know how to find you! So glad you found us."

Tears of joy. I cried like a baby when I read "Hey, Sis." I'd never been called that before.

I was surprised, excited, and could not believe the warm and positive response I received.

Since that beautiful day, I have personally met and hugged all four of my siblings. Rick and Della from Manitoba, Randy from Lacombe, and Linda, the youngest, who lives in the same city as me! My life has changed, and the sense of peace I feel is overwhelming. My lifelong desire to find my father and to be accepted has been fulfilled through his children, my siblings. Just to look at their faces and see the similarities is extraordinary. Each of them could not have been more accepting and loving, and this outcome is more than I ever imagined. I never thought it would take this long, but perhaps I was not ready until now.

Never meeting my father is still hard for me, but meeting and forming a relationship with my four siblings is a treasure, and I am so full of gratitude. God shone a light on that dark empty space, and I feel I have been reborn into a loving family that I never knew I had.

I have been blessed. I am happily married to a wonderful, loving man for thirty years this fall, and I have amazing children and grandchildren that I adore and who honor me every day.

But now I have an even greater sense of who I am. I finally feel at peace with my past.

Who knew that it would take this long to find my sense of peace? I never really knew when my prayers would be answered, but nevertheless, my prayers were constant, and my gratitude was deeply felt during my most difficult childhood and young adult life. On my journey to find my father, my faith remained strong. I remembered to be still and know that I am loved and that those things that I most desired would come to pass.

Since November, my siblings and I created a family group chat, and each day we share our lives. One day, the topic came up that I needed a nickname like the rest. The consensus was that I would be called "Angel." They said, "Because she brought us together." As I read this, I put my hand on my heart, held back a tear, and smiled the biggest smile ever! They called me an angel.

Scoliosis Strong: The Beauty Within
by Rachel Dyer

Like many sixteen year olds, I so often felt vulnerable and shy and wanted to hide from the world. Unlike most sixteen year olds, I found myself standing in just my underpants, while my surgeon and what I can only describe as a crowd of trainee doctors stood around looking at my spine, making marks where they would be cutting, and talking as if I wasn't there. I wanted the ground to open up and swallow me.

I was so embarrassed to have all these male doctors just looking at me. Well, they weren't looking directly at me so much as at my spine, but I was still so embarrassed. I asked myself why this was happening to me. What had I done so wrong in my life to deserve this? Why did I have to be here in this hospital waiting for major surgery? Why couldn't it be someone else? Back then, I had so many whys and no answers.

In May of 1984, at the tender age of fifteen, I was diagnosed with scoliosis. Unfortunately, due to the late diagnosis, it was too far advanced to do anything other than operate. My family was told that without surgery, I would be lucky if I lived into my thirties, as my curvature would press onto my heart and lungs. Back then, in the early eighties, no one really knew about scoliosis, so we had little information to go on beyond what the specialist told us. The surgery wasn't without risk either—mainly the chance of being left paralyzed, which was pretty high—but what else could we do?

Thanks to my fantastic doctor, I made it through the surgery. As it is quite gruesome, I won't describe the surgery itself, but I will tell you that

I ended up with a titanium rod in my spine, and the pain afterward was something I never want to experience again.

For the first ten days after the surgery, I had to use a Stryker bed. I weighed about ninety-eight pounds at the time, and the bed was about as wide as me, with two wings at the side for my arms. I had to lay flat on my back (no pillow), which was very interesting for a side sleeper. Then, a bar was put across my knees to stop me from raising up my legs. In order for me to turn over, another version of the bed was strapped to the top of me, with a cutout for my face. I found it terrifying, and I think this is when I developed claustrophobia. I had to eat and go to the toilet all while lying flat. How would I use the toilet while lying flat? Well, there was a piece that came out of the bottom of the bed, a potty was put on another raised underpiece, and I just had to hope my aim was good. Peeing was easy; it was doing a bowel movement that was the challenge.

During my time in hospital, I unfortunately picked up a bug, and I was so sick. I also learned the trials of trying to vomit into a kidney shaped bowl while also lying flat. I don't recommend you try it. I ended up with vomit being tipped all over me—into my hair, everywhere. And how was I going to wash my hair lying flat on this Stryker bed? It wasn't easy.

Just after I was diagnosed and before my surgery, I developed anxiety and panic attacks. During a panic attack, I would feel as if I couldn't breathe, and my heart would pound so fast and hard I thought I would pass out, or even worse, have a heart attack. I was convinced that I was going to die. I couldn't control my mind or my body and would have raging diarrhea. I would be left shaking from head to toe. It got so bad for a while that I was sleeping on the floor in my parents' bedroom, holding my mum's hand. I was terrified that if I went to sleep, I wouldn't wake up again. These attacks would stay with me until well into my forties.

A few days after surgery, I was put into a plaster—we called them plaster of Paris. The whole top half of my body was encased in plaster up over my shoulders, and it came up so high over them that, at night, my chin would rub against it in my sleep, leaving my skin quite raw. Although I hated the plaster, I also loved it because I believed that it was holding me together, and without it, my spine would fall apart. In reality, it was actually there to protect my spine while I healed. All in all, I was to spend two and a half weeks in hospital before going home, and then a few weeks after that, I would go back to school. I was to have two plasters in total—the first one for about a month, and after that, it would be exchanged for another one that I could remove to shower and would need to wear for about another five months.

Since I went to boarding school, going back would not be like returning to a regular school. It was going to be so much harder. My school was in Oxfordshire, about an hour and half drive from my home in Leicestershire, United Kingdom, and that meant I would be away from my parents and my support system. I also couldn't wear my school uniform, as my skirts would not fit over my plaster. This wasn't a bad thing, but figuring out what to wear was still a challenge. I found one pair of pants that did fit over my plaster, and they were quite trendy, so that wasn't so bad.

What was bad was the teasing. I honestly didn't think anyone would tease me about my plaster, but they did. First, I got told I looked like the Honey Monster, a character from a cereal advertisement back in the UK. My so-called friends also thought it was fun to knock on me. Yes, literally run up and knock on me because it made a strange sound, and they thought it was funny. One so-called friend thought it was fun to force me onto my back and laugh at me as I struggled to get up. As the plaster restricted my movements so much, getting up was extremely hard. On top of that, there was the humiliation that I felt. Yet I just laughed and pretended it was okay.

Roll on six years, and I was in my early twenties. To be honest, it was like the confident, courageous me had been left behind after my surgery. Before surgery, I had been the girl who would ride the roller coaster or head out on my pony without a backward glance. Now I was so self-conscious about how I looked, I felt like everyone could see my hump, my monster. I would be on vacation in Europe, enjoying the sun and the beautiful, warm ocean, but all the time, looking at the women around me with perfect bodies. I wasn't beautiful like them.

Every time I got up to go for a swim, I would put on a T-shirt so no one could see my ugly scars or my hump. I convinced myself that this is what they would all see as soon as I stood up and would laugh and talk about me behind my back, no pun intended. It would be a long time until I would feel beautiful.

I continued to struggle with self-image, anxiety, and panic attacks for so many years. During my twenties, it got so bad that I finally stopped going out with friends or even having any fun. My life was such a struggle, every single day.

I felt worthless, and although I had boyfriends, I never felt as if I was good or pretty enough for them, and there was always the nagging doubt that, because of my back, no one would ever really want me. I was always so envious of girls and women with their perfect bodies and straight backs, wearing backless tops. I could never do that. Who would want to look at me, or be around me with how I looked?

I was never diagnosed with depression, but I strongly believe now that I was depressed. There was no aftercare following my surgery, the emotional parts of the experience were never talked about, and I was never asked how I felt about it all. I don't blame anyone for this; it was just the way things were when I was younger. One thing I do believe is that if I had been offered counseling or someone to talk to about my experience and about what I saw every time I looked in the mirror, it could have saved me a lot of heartache.

Skip ahead, and I'm in my forties, happily married and living in Canada. I have a lot of my confidence back, and I feel more at peace than I ever have. Maybe that came from moving to Vancouver Island and being next to the ocean or from running my own fitness center, or because I am a co-founder of Sooke Women In Business, a group that helps support other women, not just in business, but in life and love as well. One thing I do know is that it certainly came from the amazing and supportive group of friends I now have. They've listened to me when I've cried, opened their hearts to me, and encouraged me to share my story. These ladies are my tribe, and I'm so grateful for each and every one of them.

Last, but by no means least, my peace and confidence was built up by my amazing, loving, and supportive husband, who tells me almost every day how beautiful I am. Who has held my hand and rubbed my back through every panic attack, meltdown, and tantrum, especially over the last four years, as my pain level has increased significantly. During this time, my spine has developed degeneration, arthritis, and an issue with my right leg and hip, which leaves me in a lot of pain and with a numbness down to my toes. This makes getting up every day a struggle. Despite all of that, he still loves me.

In my late forties, I did my first boudoir shoot with an amazing friend who is also a talented photographer. Boudoir photos are tasteful, classy, and elegant, but sensual and sexy as well. The photos were to be a gift to my husband as a thank you for everything he had done for me. I was terrified. Although it was my decision to do it, I still was afraid that I would be half-naked in front of my friend and that she would see my back. What would she think when she saw me? I gave her strict instructions that my back was not to be shown in any photos unless it was covered up. To prepare, we went through my wardrobe to see what clothes and underwear would work well with the shoot. Armed with those, my wedding dress, and a bottle of wine, we headed out to my husband's boat, where the shoot would take place.

Maybe it was the peacefulness of being on the boat, or the sound of the waves lapping against the hull, or the bottle of wine that I pretty much drank myself, but I found myself relaxing and enjoying the experience.

After the photos had been edited, my friend and I got together to see how they'd turned out. Imagine my surprise and shock at what I saw. Was this really me? There was no monster looking back at me, just a beautiful woman.

It's hard to explain how having these photos taken helped me to start looking at myself in a different way. Yes, my husband would tell me how beautiful I was, but I never saw it for myself until then. It gave me such a confidence boost that the following summer, I did a second shoot, and this time, I did show my back. I was still quite self-conscious, and I wasn't sure I would like what I would see, but guess what? When I got the photos back, I looked stunning. I didn't see the hump or scars. I just saw the real me. Wow. I was almost fifty, and I was just finding my inner beauty.

I have come a long way from the person who would see a monster in the mirror every day. While I do still have those days when I struggle to see the beautiful me, they are getting less and less. Now I know I am beautiful and that I am worthy of the love and friendships that I have.

Can She Come Out To Play?
by Jacqueline Carroll

The year I turned fifty-two, the little girl inside was begging me to let her out to play. I had ignored her for a very long time.

Sadness enveloped me as I came home each evening, my whole body tensing at the thought of seeing my husband and how he would disregard me this time. Who was he getting drunk and stoned with tonight? I was slowly dying inside, numb from the pain. I struggled to put one conservative, black leather pump in front of the other each day, carrying the weight of my marriage to a classic abusive narcissist when I was thirty-three. I often compromised many of my foundational core values and silenced my voice by not standing up for myself. I was always settling in my personal relationships and over giving to fill emotional voids. I allowed other people to set my worth. I was a magnet for the opportunists, users, and narcissists. I made it easy for them as I showed people how to treat me.

Along with the little girl inside, the other voices chattering in my head were now constant. *You've settled for this long! You don't need that! Better yet, you made your bed! You can't even do this right! Who else would want you anyway? This is as good as it gets, honey!*

I settled for where I was and who I was with. I was in an empty marriage with a man whose world revolved around himself, his wants, and his friends. My values were compromised so much that I didn't even know who I truly was anymore. I was spiraling into a dark hole; a place I wasn't sure that I could climb out of. During this spiral, I became numb. I was comatose and my world was getting darker and darker.

This comatose state was absolutely exhausting. I was hiding behind a mask. I just went through the motions. I held a senior executive position that required me to be on my game every day, and I could not reveal my vulnerabilities, my weaknesses. My husband always had to be surrounded by his people. There were visitors at my house constantly, and I continued to be the gracious host, but I was guarded with most people coming into my life. The effort of hiding behind all that was grueling.

In my misery and despair, every now and then I would see a glimmer of hope. I had put myself out there with total strangers when I joined a wellness challenge group. The sessions were tapping into my skills and potential. This optimism was showing up more and more often. There was also a voice inside me asking, "When are you going to take charge of your life?" It wasn't the usual busy chatter but a soft, childlike voice almost pleading with me. "When are you going to do something?" As months went by in my fifty-second year, the voice was becoming more insistent. A determined voice filled with loving kindness that I didn't usually allow myself to hear. The voice of the little girl inside of me who wanted to come out to play!

On the day I was born, God gifted me a limited time on this earth. I don't know how many days that is, but I know that I won't get a refund on the days that I haven't lived my life to the fullest. Many evenings, as I watched the sunset from my deck, I reminded myself of this.

In honoring the gift of my life, I could not ignore the pleas any longer.

As I looked to my future, I could not imagine continuing to live in this state. In our ice-cold bedroom absent of any connection, in my mind, I toiled over and over again how I was going to take charge of my life. I was dying inside. My heart and soul were so broken I didn't know how I could ever recover. I knew I was going to succumb to disease at some point, mentally or physically, if things didn't change. Deep in my heart, I knew where I needed to be, but the real struggles were really believing it and figuring out how I was going to get there. I absolutely needed a plan.

Up until then, I was a "how to" addict. I had read almost every self-help book on the market. Titles including, *How To Have The Perfect Body, Lose 20 Pounds In 20 Days, Spice Up Your Relationships, Home Renovations 101,* just to name a few. I even read, three weeks after my wedding, *Now*

That I Am Married, Why Do I Still Feel Like This? Name it, I probably read it. I became a master "do-it-yourselfer." All the reading didn't help much, because I hadn't allowed myself to believe that I was worthy and deserving of anything better. The acquired knowledge never translated into my life. The insanity of doing the same thing over and over again and expecting different results was my own madness.

Where to start? The universe was showing me some things at this point because I was more receptive to receiving. There was a shift happening. I knew I had to do more things for myself. But what? I reached deep inside myself to figure out what I was passionate about. Beyond my corporate life, I knew I had skills and talents to share with people who needed them. Opportunities presented themselves, and I began volunteering with a local women's charity—a volunteer-driven organization that increases the confidence and self-esteem of women facing barriers to employment by providing them with one-on-one service to help them create a work-appropriate wardrobe. This work ignited a spark in me, and I thrived working with these women.

Within a month, I attended a large women's event. I listened to amazing, empowering women sharing their stories. I was in awe of their tragedies and triumphs. That day, I had a personal mini session with a doctor who specialized in communicating with the subconscious mind, using kinesiology to discover how one's unhealthy beliefs affect the body both physically and mentally. She asked me, "What do you want to work on today?"

I started to feel uncomfortable and a bit nervous. So, I skirted around the question. "I am struggling with my weight," I replied.

That matter was quickly addressed, and she pressed on. "What else is there?"

At this point, I became much more uncomfortable, feeling trapped. The little girl inside was much more vocal now. "Tell her!" she screamed.

Again, I avoided the question and replied almost sheepishly, "My relationships."

What happened in the next thirty seconds changed my life. She looked me square in the eyes and said, "He doesn't give two shits about you, honey!"

She may as well have hit me on the side of the head with a two-by-four. My first thought was, how dare she say that to me! But I was busted. She didn't tell me anything that I didn't already know inside, but now I was exposed. No more hiding behind the mask.

That day was my turning point. Before I got home that night, I made a promise to myself: "This is not how my story is going to end!" With that promise, I went into action mode with more clarity and determination than I'd ever had before. I had had enough. I took charge of saving myself and the little girl inside. She was screaming with glee by now. "Hallelujah! Let's do this!"

Our transformational journey began.

I had given up my own power as a woman and settled for so much less than I deserved for far, far too long. The first thing I had to address was my failing long-term marriage. There was nothing left to salvage. I had nothing more to give emotionally or financially. I deserved to reconnect with my family and friends who had been alienated from me.

I deserved more than the covert, narcissistic, emotional abuse, as well as the alcohol and drug use that I put up with. I deserved a real, loving partner. Someone who shared goals and dreams with me. I deserved to matter to someone, to be a priority, and not have my feelings, needs, and wants disregarded. I created my exit plan, quietly putting my affairs in order. Deep inside, I was scared as hell but also really excited. I gained the strength and courage to take back my own power and reclaim my voice. In all that, I was saving my life. There was no turning back.

Within six weeks of attending the women's event and two weeks before Christmas, I ended my marriage. I could not bear the thought of spending another holiday, much less another day together. This was all about me now. I felt like one hundred thousand pounds were lifted from my shoulders and my world. The numbness was fading. I was waking up from the coma.

Shortly after I made the announcement, I took my dog, MJ, to the off-leash park. I still get emotional remembering the sights and the sounds of that day. I couldn't remember the last time I had allowed myself to feel what was going on around me. Until that point, I had been consumed by my sadness. Now, the sun was brilliantly reflecting off the snow. The energy was electric, even magical. I felt joy in the park. The dogs were giddy with excitement, children were playing, people smiling and laughing, birds were singing. Despite what I had gone through a few hours before, I was easily caught up in it. Before I left the park, a protective presence came over me. I sensed that my guardian angels were watching me. I knew then I was not alone, and I was protected. Everything was going to be just fine.

Getting through the following twenty months was like a roller coaster ride, but a beacon of light shone on me, guiding me to the finish line. I had many balls in the air. I was navigating the end of my marriage and, at the same time, reclaiming my own power and my true, authentic self. The more I owned my power, the less control he had. I had to be strategic with every word that came out of my mouth, every action I took. I knew exactly who I was dealing with, and I did what I had to do to get to the end zone. An added challenge was that my emotions were scattered—the grief over the end of a twenty plus year relationship, along with fear, joined by elation and excitement about what my new world would look like.

My personal growth was now catapulting. I set out on my healing journey with conviction, and I was unstoppable. I was teachable and coachable. I participated in workshops and seminars. I read. I listened. It was the new me, free of the mask, who started to show up at work each day. I built a new tribe, surrounding myself with empowering people who feed my soul. I worked with my coach, identifying and smashing false beliefs that no longer served me. I embarked on many "firsts." I learned how to truly love myself and honor the little girl inside me.

It has been four and a half years since that magical day in the park. I am still an amazing work in progress. I continue to invest in myself every day. I am living the best version of me, honoring my true, authentic self. I do believe with every fiber of my being that my value is infinite, and I am deserving of the best. I am free of the pain and sadness; I am unrecognizable to my past. My new life, filled with adventures, is so rich that I cannot put a price tag on it. It did cost me my old life, and I wouldn't have it any other way. The little girl in me has come out to play.

How I Found My Wings
by Daphne A. McDonagh

To this day, I feel like throwing up and the right side of my head hurts every time I hear the breaking glass and the bending metal of two vehicles colliding. I choose not to remember much of the crash that changed my life, and I am grateful that most of that memory has been blocked. For years, I have been told that I broke the passenger window with my head when the truck smashed into the front end of the car. My memory has given me snippets from that night, and I now know that the head injury came from when my head bounced off the concrete. I was left lying in the middle of the intersection when the vehicles stopped spinning. My mother and I were involved in this near-fatal car accident when I was a teenager.

Since then, I've learned that the universe always provides me with exactly what I need at exactly the right time. I love how wonderful synchronicities appear daily to assist me in discovering what my true purpose in life is. My healing box is filled with metamorphic tools that others have shared with me over the last twenty years. Step by step, I realize that I have all the power within to allow my body to heal.

In reference to my accident, many people have said, "Isn't it wonderful how such a tragic experience turned into such a wonderful gift?" I can honestly say that I did not realize at the time the bigger purpose for me being here, but I simply needed to go through what I did to be able to assist others from a place of truth.

My parents told me the ambulance attendants radioed the hospital telling them that I was DOA (dead on arrival). My parents, however, fought for my life; they were not willing to let go of their only daughter. They knew I was not done and would not let the doctors harvest my organs that night.

My wings grew and flew back from the heavens the moment my parents decided they were not ready to live without me. There was a bigger purpose for me being here, and I needed to finish my job before I checked out.

Even before the accident, I always knew I had a gift to help animals and people feel better, and that was the norm for me. I did not know that those abilities didn't come naturally to others. I could place my hands on an injury and magically take the pain away. Little did I know, it would take me over twenty years to figure out what that purpose was. Back then, I was a teenager trapped in a hospital after serious physical trauma, and I didn't have the energy or capacity to think about any purpose in life other than surviving. I am truly amazed how my subconscious protected me at this time. I am grateful I do not consciously remember the hard parts, like when they unplugged me from the life support and were not expecting me to live, or when the doctors told my parents that I was going to remain in a coma for the rest of my life. "Daphne's prognosis is guarded due to the neurological injuries which she has sustained" is what the neurological team wrote in a letter to my parents. The doctors did not think that I was ever going to be able to function as a human being again. Little did they know that I had a different plan!

I wouldn't wish what I went through on anyone else. I was angry it happened and pissed off at the world. Going from an athletic teenager that played sports and rode my horse twice a day to not even being able to go to the bathroom by myself was aggravating, to say the least. I was bedridden and could only go somewhere if I had help getting out of bed and I was being pushed in a wheelchair. I was embarrassed and ashamed that I could not do simple tasks. My heart was sad, and I didn't know how I could go on. There was a piece of hair shaved from where they put the shunt in my head to drain the fluid when I was still on life support. I felt ugly and was very depressed because, not only was I dealing with constant pain, but my left eyelid was barely open and my eye turned out. For a fifteen-year-old girl, this was a hard pill to swallow.

I had many therapists and was on such a schedule that it drove me crazy. I would have to rest after each therapy session to allow my body to heal. I did not realize at the time that sleep was the best medicine.

Stubbornness and perseverance guided me back. Relearning how to walk and talk helped me to appreciate life that much more. As a young athlete, I took for granted stamina and coordination. I never realized how many muscles were actually needed to be used or activated to go from a sitting to a standing position.

Growing up, my nickname had been Motor Mouth. Now, not being able to talk really pissed me off. I knew what I was wanting to say, but it was like there was a malfunction at the junction and the words would not come out when I wanted them to.

I sat alone in the dining room of the pediatric ward in the Glenrose Hospital. I asked myself, "Is this really how I want to spend the rest of my life?" I was done eating another tasteless meal and was tired of being treated like a baby. Being fifteen, I had no clue of what was to come, but I knew in my heart that I needed to make the choice to get my butt in gear and start my healing journey. It was then I realized that if I wanted more from my life, I would need to do the work required to get me the heck out of dodge. It was then I began to learn the valuable lesson of work for reward.

I love the reaction I get when I say that I was in the hospital for only eight months. To many, that is a lifetime. Considering the injuries I sustained, eight months was really a simple drop of water in the ocean of my life.

After that moment in the dining room, I made sure to put the extra effort into each of my therapy sessions. I would even do extra leg lifts while eating my meals to help strengthen my legs faster. I was done riding in a wheelchair and wanted to find my feet again. Five months after I made that choice, I walked out of the Glenrose Rehabilitation Hospital, emerging from my cocoon. Spreading my wings confidently to fly to unexpected places or into hidden caverns to discover the treasures of each new day. Looking back now, I can say that rehabilitation was the best learning experience I've ever had. It has guided me to be the person I am today: understanding, devoted, persistent and conscientious.

I thought that completing high school and working in the real world was my next step. Little did I know that working as a subservient waitress and shift worker would suck.

I don't know if it was God or Google that helped me find the rehabilitation practitioner program. Either way, *voilà*! I thought I had found my calling. I was a person with a disability, and I could help other people who had disabilities get better too. After two intense years of full-time college classes, I graduated from Grant MacEwan with first-class standing with my rehabilitation practitioner diploma.

I loved assisting people with learning skills to help them live and work independently in society. When people asked me what my job was, I told them I empowered people not to need me anymore. After eight years in this field, I began to see the whole truth. Many people who have disabilities do not want to get better, and really who was I kidding, I wasn't even taking care of myself. I was pretending to be fine and trying to help everyone else fix their issues, while I ignored my own, sweeping them under the rug of despair.

The universe works in magical ways and has blessed me with my purpose of being a wife, a mother, a business owner, and a conduit for others. Once I was able to dissolve my trapped energies and physical pain, I realized my wings were bigger than I ever thought and that I could fly farther than I ever imagined. I began to see the world on a grander scale.

The possibilities are endless when it comes to crystal therapy. What started out as me carrying some magnets in my pockets has now turned into my full-time business of Daphne's Healing Hands. Assisting others to balance, restore, and rejuvenate their energies by using crystal, cold laser, and different energy therapies brings me such joy. Creating custom pieces of healing jewelry for animals and people specific to their needs is mind blowing to some. I love seeing the smile on someone's face when the pain magically disappears in their neck after putting on one of the necklaces I have created.

My heart is full when I empower others, be it animals or people, to dissolve their stuck energies, both emotional and physical. One of my first examples of this was when Cali, a friend's cat, was getting older and showing signs of joint and arthritic pains. Cali was getting up there in age and the owner did not know how to assist. She booked me for an appointment to see what I could do to help her cat. After only two sessions of cold laser therapy and energy work, Cali was running around like a kitten again. After the second treatment, the owner jumped up from a sitting position off the couch without having to use her cane to assist. I realized in this perfect moment how much animals want to help their owner live without pain. Animals are selfless. They will take our pain away from us so we do not need to feel it. I love it when people come to me asking me to help their animals. After a little investigating, it really is surprising how many times these physical conditions that are showing up in the animals can be linked back to their owners.

I recently was asked to go and help a horse that had a front foot concern, but there was no medical diagnosis that the veterinarians could come up with. After some conversation with his owner and helping this beautiful being to unwind from the stress and dis-ease that he seemed to be facing, I discovered that his owner had a foot concern as well. Once I was able to assist the owner to release and let go of the emotional ties that she had been carrying in her foot, you can only guess what happened for the horse. Well yes, the front foot issues it had been carrying for years magically disappeared.

Truly, what I love doing most, out of all the different modalities I practice, is distant therapy sessions. These allow me to treat animals and people worldwide. There was a dog in Europe that needed my assistance after going through back surgery. Only one week after treatments began, the dog was up and running around like a brand-new puppy. The owners were astounded at the amazing results.

One of my human clients moved from a state of agitation and physical exhaustion to a place of feeling grounded and calm after her distant therapy sessions. She was more focused and able to create again.

When I do these treatments, I place a picture of the person or animal that I'm treating under a sacred geometry tool called a sun ring, with a clear and a smoky quartz laying over it, as well as the infrared cold laser and triple pyramid. I send the vibration with healing intent, and the results are out of this world.

I am a healer.

I am aware that my contributions help others.

I am grateful they allow me to share my gifts and abilities.

Witnessing animals and people raise their vibration to release and let go of their stuck energies is magical. Being the conduit for this is breathtaking. Seeing them find their own wings again is truly transformational. Many of these magical beings' bodies have been in fight or flight mode for so long that they do not know how to relax. It is so rewarding for me to see a person who is visibly uncomfortable and metaphorically going nine hundred miles an hour at the start of a treatment to smiling an hour later and being at peace within themselves, ready to take on anything that is thrown their way.

Yes, sometimes life is difficult, but it really is all about perception. I believe we each can choose how we see our difficulties. I find when people are given options for a different way to look at things and embrace a new beginning, life gets way more exciting. It really isn't about fighting for what we want. When we can release and let go of what is no longer serving us, we can trust and allow the universe to have our backs.

I am grateful every day I wake up, as it means I still have a purpose to fulfill, and I am aware that everything will work out exactly as it is supposed to. I no longer worry when or how things are going to happen. When I tap into source and channel, I do not need to think about what I am doing. To feel the flowing movement of the wings I've been given, and to take flight as the healer I am.

Epilogue

I sincerely hope that you enjoyed *Sacred Hearts Rising: Finding Your Wings*. Women and men have already stepped forward to contribute to Sacred Hearts Rising Book #3, and I invite you to consider if you'd like to be one of them.

I hope that what you've read here has touched your heart somehow. As you immersed yourself in each story, you may have noticed yourself stepping into the shoes of that person. That you felt what she or he was feeling. Empathy is a powerful thing. Reading about the lives of these brave human beings may have reminded you of similar experiences in your life, and you may have noticed old memories bubbling to the surface. Or perhaps you just enjoyed reading about their determination to accept and change their lives.

If old (or recent) memories surfaced and you found this disturbing, I encourage you to seek help in dealing with them. Talk to someone you trust. This could be your doctor, a friend, your minister, or priest. It might mean calling a sexual abuse or domestic violence hotline, seeking spiritual guidance, or searching on the Internet for what you need. Above all, please continue asking for help until somebody finally listens to you.

One resource I can offer is the Sacred Hearts Newsletter found at www.sacredheartsrising.com. Please sign up and join. Each month, we feature authors from *Sacred Hearts Rising: Breaking the Silence One Story at a Time* and *Sacred Hearts Rising: Finding Your Wings*. You will be able to contact them from the information they have provided.

As a survivor of multiple traumas, I have used many different modes of therapy, each one helping me in a way that I needed at that time. Whatever it is, don't be afraid to take that first step. And whatever your journey may be, I wish you the love, success, and healing you need.

If you're feeling called to share your story, please send me a note at:
spiritcreek@xplornet.com,
or visit the website at *www.sacredheartsrising.com.*

Brenda Hammon

About the Authors

Shey Henning

A passionate pursuer of Jesus, a mother of two incredible adults and four wonderful stepchildren. Shey is an acclaimed vocalist who studied voice with the Brandon Conservatory of Music starting at the age of thirteen. Shey then continued on with her music and went into a bachelor of education program at Brandon University. Her true passion was found in the financial world as a successful financial coach, and with that passion, she rose quickly and is seated on an advisory board for women in North America. With her husband by her side as her partner in life and in business, Shey knows life has just began and they are unstoppable.

Laureen Nowlan-Card

Laureen Nowlan-Card has been an advocate for women and children her whole adult life. Her natural passion for advocacy led to a successful career as a courtroom lawyer for over twenty years. Five years ago, she decided that she wanted to support women in a more proactive and personal way. She became a certified transformational life coach and then the first Canadian certified in emotional liberation therapy. Laureen guides women to release their self-doubt and limiting beliefs and to work with their emotions so they can attain increased joy and peace, rather than continuing to be overwhelmed by difficult emotions. Laureen is also the founder of Victoria WomanSpeak and Victoria GirlSpeak—public speaking training, where she is proud to help women and girls unleash the brilliance of their voices and ideas. Believing deeply in community and that "we were never meant to do all this alone," Laureen also facilitates women's sharing circles and has founded The Oasis for Women.

Jennifer Strachan

Jennifer is a small business owner who is passionate about her work and her clients, with over twenty-five years in the beauty industry. She has learned that beauty runs much deeper than physical appearances. She helps empower women by helping them embrace their own unique and imperfect beauty. She is purposeful in assisting women to understand the invaluable importance of self-love. She volunteers her time mentoring and inspiring others by sharing her experience, giving others the gift of hope.

Jennifer decided over six years ago to accept help for her disease of addiction; instead of continuing to kill herself with drugs, she needed to make significant life changes and take responsibility for her life, and that's exactly what she did.

Jennifer is a devoted partner, mom, stepmom, sister, and auntie to those she cherishes most. Today she lives in gratitude and the miracle of the moment.

Sheryl Rist

Dr. Sheryl Rist is the owner of Balanced Lifestyle and Wellness. She has been an Alberta registered acupuncturist since 2001, and a doctor of natural medicine since 2006. As a dedicated, intuitive healing professional, Sheryl's heart and mind are always in her work. As a true healer, Sheryl melds many modalities and spiritual practices. Sheryl is grateful for everything in her life and uses her difficult past experiences to help others come out of the darkness and into the light to lead joyful, healthy lives. Sheryl's love of life is evident in her hearty laugh and her exuberant energy. Sheryl is a humble, hardworking visionary who is creating change to benefit others, the world, and future generations, all while soaking up every ounce of life with her twin boys.

Kurtis Clay

Kurtis Clay is a voice-over artist and has owned his own recording studio since the age of sixteen. He has worked since that time with voice talent Anthony Reece, honing his skills and perfecting his craft.

He currently resides in Edmonton, Alberta, with his parents, Don and Marta, but is originally from Little Rock, Arkansas. Kurtis considers himself Canadian, since he moved to Alberta at the tender age of seven.

His life's ambition is to become the voice that people readily recognize, work in the video gaming industry (which he has already worked on two such projects), and teach people throughout the world about living on the autism spectrum, especially with Asperger's syndrome.

Kit Fraser

Kit Fraser is an aspiring song-writing musician with a passionate heart. Though always enamored by piano and poetry, much lifetime would pass before she finally determined to accept her musical calling. Studying piano in childhood, her instructor publicly expressed amazement at Kit's ability to play classical music without being able to hear all the notes. Embarrassing for Kit, yet incredibly uplifting, at the same time. Defective hearing was often a disparaging impairment, but along with other seemingly insurmountable obstacles, human challenge eventually became a driving strength, allowing the evolution of intuitive creation. Over time, Kit was inspired to embrace her broken spirit, harness her power, and focus on forgiveness and love. Now, on a mission of beautiful hope, Kit Fraser is surely rising with her sisters and brothers, as messengers of love and compassion, calling unto the emerging consciousness of our world.

Elizabeth Gagnon

Elizabeth Jean Olivia Gagnon is an author, the founder of Miss Liz's Tea Parties, and a changemaker.

A survivor of abuse and grief, Liz is making change in the world by creating magical events where people come together to share their stories of trauma and triumph. Liz is the founder of the Tea Bag Story Award and Miss Liz's Tea Parties. Since 2015, these events have grown exponentially and raised over $5,000 for women's transition houses, sexual abuse services, Parkinson's resources, and bereaved family services. Liz also hosts an annual Christmas open house for single moms, their children, and the homeless. She is heavily involved with Bereaved Families of Ontario-Cornwall and is a member of the Community Action Network Against Abuse.

Liz has been a contributing author in 'Canada 150 Stories' and the first *Sacred Hearts Rising* anthology. Writing has been part of her healing journey. In 2011, Liz was recognized as a living example of never giving up when she was presented with the Hope and Resilience Award from the Canadian Mental Health Association.

Liz is committed to breaking the stigma around mental health issues. Learn more about Liz at *www.misslizsteaparties.com*.

Patricia Dalgleish

Patricia Dalgleish grew up on a farm and is the youngest of nine. She has been married for twenty-five years and is proud to have been able to be a mom and stepmom to five kids and manage a blended family that has put the kids first. She is also a proud grandma to seven grandkids.

In the past twenty years, she has managed to work together with her husband in their telecommunications business managing bookkeeping and behind the scenes tasks.

In January 2010, she was diagnosed with breast cancer. Along the journey of healing, she found psychosomatic (psyche: mind, soma: body) healing.

It allowed her to grow emotionally and accept her path with the momentum to move forward and enjoy life. Now she is on a path to build her own business and to empower others to begin their journey to heal. She completed the first certificate in 2013, and certificate IV in 2017 in psychosomatic therapy.

Carol Black

From very early on in her life Carol has been interested in learning about different spiritual beliefs and searching for a path that would help her understand her life. She keeps this an ongoing process—the door is never closed!

She is a partner in a home staging and decorating company, which allows her to have a wonderful creative outlet. She also enjoys spending time with her close friends and family with a good glass of wine and interesting conversation.

Carol is a very proud mother of two well-rounded adults and Nana to two wonderful grandsons and two grand dogs. She has lived most of her life in Edmonton but is now enjoying her life by the sea in White Rock, British Columbia.

Bonnie Nicole

Bonnie was raised in small-town Fort Langley, British Columbia, and grew up on a fifty-acre farm close to all her adoptive family and biological mom. Bonnie spent most of her life thinking she was unworthy and struggled with body image and addictions. She bounced from one dysfunctional relationship to the next, until she woke up one day and said, "No more." Bonnie now puts her effort in ending the cycles of abuse and trauma in her family and extends the help to the public. She runs Facebook challenges to get women supporting one another daily. Bonnie lives in Abbotsford, British Columbia, with her children and pets. She has proven to many that no matter your story is, it is worth sharing, and if willing to share it, just know it will help someone who needed to hear it.

Rika Harris

After raising her family of five, Rika turned her energies to discovering her next passion and role in life. Ready to start all over, she utilized her counseling training to become a compassionate listener. This has been developed and refined over the last twenty years, and she uses this concept to connect people with their hidden stories releasing pain, shame, or trauma by making them feel heard and understood.

Helping others to find their voices and feel valued and validated lights her up, and this light and love are reflected back to her clients. She passionately believes that we can make a difference in our world by connecting heart to heart and being sacred mirrors for each other.

You can find her on Facebook in her group "Awaken Your Voice" or you can contact her by email at *rika.nurturer@gmail.com.*

Sheree Agerskov

An entrepreneur for thirty years, Sheree has been a grain farmer, co-owned a computer business, and operated a retail store. Her current passion is building a business in Strathmore, Alberta, all natural and organic, using ancient methods of hair removal. She proudly specializes in sugared Brazilians and threaded brows. She is co-owner of Langdon Women Talk as well as a volunteer and director with Women Talk Canada, a platform where ordinary women share their extraordinary stories, creating deeper connections, and a more meaningful life.

Having spent the last forty plus years on a journey of emotional and spiritual healing, Sheree is recreating herself and her life. Very passionate about her personal and emotional growth, she has explored many paths to overcome severe childhood trauma and abuse, teenage addictions, and domestic abuse. From self-loathing and self-sabotage, to radical self-acceptance and self-love, she is ready to share her story, shame free, with the intention of empowering herself and others. Learn more at *www.LivBeautifulSugaring.com.*

Alexis Ellis

Alexis is an inspirational speaker and contributing author to the Sacred Hearts anthology series. A hard worker who is always willing to help others, Alexis has embarked on her speaking career to help her community and to lead by example.

Alexis lived with her true self hidden for most of her life. Then, at the age of thirty-six, she began her courageous journey through gender change, reassignment surgery, and finally being able to live authentically as her real self. Alexis is on a mission to share her experience as a transgender woman because she believes that it is time for society to fully accept transgender people. With suicide rates among the transgender community being extremely high, Alexis knows her message is important. Her story is one of courage and walking her talk. Alexis's greatest wish is for all people to be free to be their true selves and she hopes that sharing her story will inspire others!

Tracy Childs

Tracy Childs likes to keep busy on her farm in rural Alberta. She loves to laugh there as much as she can with her husband and two daughters, as well as the dogs, cats, and horses. She is active in the community, volunteers with several local organizations, and is affectionately known as "The Trophy Lady" because she also runs iMaGiNaTioN Engraving—a shop that supplies local clubs with trophies, plaques, and custom awards.

She still struggles with self-harm, anxiety, and depression but has found sharing this story to be a very healing experience.

This is her first published piece of writing. You can find more of her creative endeavours at her Facebook page: *www.facebook.com/iMaGiNaTioN363* or contact her by email at *imaginationengraving@yahoo.ca.*

Holly Holmberg

One of Canada's leading animal and intuitive professional essential oil therapists, Holly Holmberg is an international keynote aromatherapy speaker, Canadian navy veteran, former Olympic-level biathlete and contributing author to the number one international bestseller *Sacred Hearts Rising: Breaking the Silence One Story at a Time.*

She is the light worker and clinical aromatherapist behind Quantum Soul Mechanic: vibrational soul thread reconnection, Red Horse Aromatherapy: therapeutic essential oils and blends, and Enchanted Forest Adventure Retreats: reconnecting you to Mother Earth and your earthly vibe.

Holly's in-the-trenches coaching style teaches others how to use their life experiences to find their power within and focus on where they are going to, not what they are going through.

Find out more at *www.quantumsoulmechanic.com.*

Laura-Lee Harrison

Laura-Lee Harrison is a woman of many talents. As a mother of a two year old, she has her hands full if that wasn't enough, she has an online health and wellness business, is a freelance makeup artist, special effects artist, esthetician, singer, energy healer, animal lover, and an intuitive. Laura-Lee wears many shoes.

Committed to moving forward, her current efforts are focused on creating another company and a loving, fulfilled life for herself and her family.

Marta Clay

With twenty years of experience in the financial industry, Marta Clay is a senior vice president partner with Primerica Financial Services. As members of the Financial Independence Council with Primerica, she and her husband received the company's highest award in 2017; they were inducted onto the company's wall of fame.

Originally from Little Rock, Arkansas, Marta currently resides in Edmonton, Alberta, with her husband, Don, and son, Kurtis. They enjoy traveling extensively and spending quality time with family and the friends they've acquired since moving to Canada.

Marta's passion is to help people's dreams come true. She accomplishes this through her family's financial services endeavor. Also, as a natural planner and organizer, she's spent many years designing once-in-a-lifetime events for momentous occasions in her friends' and family's lives through her company, Memories Created.

Find out more at *www.memoriescreated.ca.*

Wendy Walsh

Wendy has lived in Spruce Grove, Alberta, with her rescue pup, Remington, for the last ten years but grew up in Edmonton, Alberta. Her ultimate goal is to find herself finally living in her happy place, British Columbia, surrounded by animals.

She has worked in the health-care industry for the past twenty-seven years and currently works as an administrative assistant in the health records department of a local hospital.

Her true passion is her love for animals, and she would someday like to own and run an animal rescue and sanctuary to give all those who need it a loving and safe home.

Wendy's hobbies include traveling, camping, being outdoors, and spending time with friends and family.

Nancy (Nance) Chaplin

Nancy (Nance) Chaplin is known as Exponential Joy, for she truly has learned to live an exponentially joyful life. Trauma was her story. Joy is her life. She is the founder and CEO of Exponential Joy. Nancy is a certified yoga teacher, spiritual response therapist (SRT), Reiki practitioner, aromatherapist and light worker. She uses the many modalities of healing to help clear and balance your energies. Her purpose and passion is to help as many people as possible through her exciting webinar series "Make Your Magic Happen" launching in 2019.

Stephanie Leach

Stephanie was born and raised in Vancouver, British Columbia, then moved to Calgary, Alberta, for twenty-four years and moved back to Vancouver Island in 2014. She is married and has an amazing stepson, Jay.

Her life mission is about learning, growing, and being the best she can be. She describes life as a game of snakes and ladders; sometimes we are up and other times down, it is how we deal with the down times and get back up that define us.

Since 1998, Stephanie has had a vision of speaking and writing about overcoming obstacles and adversities, and she is now at a place in life where she is ready to live that dream.

She graduated from the Erickson College coaching program in 2014 and will be starting as a WomanSpeak circle leader in Nanaimo, British Columbia, in November 2018. She sees WomanSpeak as a more supportive place to learn the art of speaking because it provides an alternative for women to harness the power of their feminine energy, rather than hide or deny it, as they speak up to lead and effect change. WomanSpeak is located throughout North America and in seven countries.

Find out more at *www.womanspeak.com.*

Jeanine LeBlanc

Jeanine LeBlanc began Patch Animal Rescue after moving to the eastern shore of Nova Scotia, Canada. She shares her home and love with several sick animals and provides shelter and food for several others. As an independent woman, Jeanine also built All-Star Painting and Decorating, which successfully grew to afford the cost of loving them.

Jeanine is also working at having her own book, "The Flow," published, of which she began to write during the time of her addiction. Rising power over mental and physical abuse, drug and gambling addictions, near-sudden death, and wrongful imprisonment, Jeanine shares how she finds the flow which carries her from near death into a purposeful and beautiful life. Over the cold winter months, she also works at fine wildlife sculpting over the inside loving walls of her quaint country home.

Sue Ferreira

After forty years practicing as an anesthesiologist in the invisible world of the operating room, for her second act, Sue Ferreira, after a gray divorce at the age of sixty, surprised herself by becoming an entrepreneur, with a passion for helping women grow their businesses with video and the cutting-edge tools of the web.

Living in rapidly changing times, many women are starting businesses later in life, but marketing has changed dramatically in the past decade with video becoming your most powerful tool. Video gives you attention and visibility, the keys to success today, yet many, especially women, have challenges embracing and benefiting from video.

Knowing she can make you camera and tech confident so you can grow your influence, impact, and income, Sue created Wisdom To Wealth Mastery, enabling you to take your wisdom to the world with video.

Susan Janzen

Susan Janzen was born in Calgary, and raised in Edmonton, Alberta. As a child, she lived in foster care, in an all-girls convent, and off and on with her mother until, at age fifteen, she left home to go it alone.

She graduated high school, got married, had two children, and was a professional singer and recording artist for eighteen years. After her divorce in 1982, Susan was honored to represent the City of Edmonton as the first local "Klondike Kate" for two years while raising her two small children. She remarried in 1988, returned to school, and graduated with a bachelor of education degree and taught special needs children for six years.

In 2003, she became a licensed realtor, and today, she is a proud mother of five, grandmother of eight, and a great grandma, too! Despite her rough childhood and the challenges she's faced, Susan remains optimistic and full of gratitude.

Rachel Dyer

Rachel was born in Leicester in the United Kingdom and is the youngest of four children. Rachel married her Canadian husband in 2006 and immigrated to Canada.

She is co-owner of a fitness center in Sooke, British Columbia. She is also co-founder and president of Sooke Women In Business and loves to see women empowering other women.

Rachel was diagnosed with scoliosis at the age of fifteen and underwent major spine surgery at sixteen. She hopes to raise awareness of scoliosis and the importance of early detection.

Rachel lives in British Columbia and loves to spend time with her husband and dogs, Oscar and Hank.

Jacqueline Carroll

Jacqueline Carroll, CEO of Carroll Consulting Services, speaker, author and magic-maker.

Finding herself in her fifties unhappily married to an abusive narcissist and facing a bleak future, Jacqueline made a promise to herself that "this is not how my story is going to end." This promise led her on a transformational journey of exponential growth. Jacqueline gathered the courage to take back her power and reclaim her authentic self. Since then, she has manifested and created the richest life filled with optimism, joy, gratitude, and adventure.

Friends call her Jacqueline 2.0 because she is living the second half of her life to the fullest. Since retiring from a thirty-six-year career in education, Jacqueline has been following her passion, supporting and mentoring others and saying "yes" to her dreams and desires. She is CEO at Carroll Consulting Services, sits on a charity board, and volunteers extensively.

Jacqueline is a resilient, courageous, kind, and passionate woman who now owns her worth in the world. Jacqueline is on a mission to inspire others to make magic happen in their lives!

Daphne A. McDonagh

For many years, Daphne has helped both animals and people to let go of unnecessary energetic baggage they are carrying. She helps them to live a life on purpose and without pain, both physical and emotional. Daphne especially loves assisting pets and their owners' transition through the releasing process together.

Drawing from her diverse educational background, including, rehabilitation, animal science, along with crystal and cold laser therapies, she balances, restores, and rejuvenates energies.

This is her second published piece of writing. You can learn more about her services at *www.daphneshealinghands.com.*

Email her at *daphne@daphneshealinghands.com.*

A Note From the Curator on the Artist's Work

Renowned artist, Riëtte Delport, created the beautiful cover painting for *Sacred Hearts Rising: Finding Your Wings* when she heard about the anthology and the topics of the stories that would be shared.

As with the stories within these pages, her art work speaks volumes about people and the everyday challenges placed in their paths.

Thank you, Riëtte, for seeing the true beauty of *Sacred Hearts Rising* in your exquisite work of art.

The artist, Riëtte Delport, has been creating these beautiful, fascinating and intricate creations for almost a decade now. Her passion to be creative is reflected on every piece she works on, and the growth in her work is something to behold. She also endeavors to grow into her passion by regularly attending workshops and courses on a personal level to even further enhance this special gift of hers she so humbly shares with us.

An artist that creates paintings like our beloved ©Rut only has so much time on her hands. Because of demand, there is always pressure to produce. Her art is not superficial, and is a real tangible and self-evident investment. The quality, and passion, that these original works of art are created with, sets this amazing artist apart from her peers.

About the Cover Painting Artist

Riëtte Delport

©RuT ArT portrays intimate portraits of angels that speak, inspire and comfort. The Artist Riëtte Delport resides in the picturesque town of Mossel Bay about 400 kilometers east of Cape Town, South Africa. Riëtte draws her inspiration from creating each piece of art from the story of Ruth in the Bible. Ruth was an impeccable woman—loving, kind and full of compassion toward everyone surrounding her. Ruth was loyal, and she most of all loved God dearly.

Riëtte paints some of her art pieces with the absence of facial features hoping that each person would see something of themselves in the piece. It is your interpretation that makes each piece of art unique and personal.

©RuT draws her inspiration from God, angels, her amazing husband and two wonderful children. She enjoys working with many different types of mediums, which include clay and, wood portrait. She recently started painting on furniture.

What best describes where she is and what she feels is the following: each day we are born again. What we do today is what matters most.

When she is not painting, she spends her time with her family, enjoying reading and playing the cello.

The Facebook page, Rut Artist, mostly includes posts of her lastest and newest original creations of ©RuT. There are also some new creations in different genres that flow out of ©RuT ArT as works of art.

Another Facebook page is ©RutCreations. This page features posts of all the smaller items in die Rut brand. These creations include images of original artwork created on products like pendants, gift cards, notepads, brooches, earrings, keyrings, and many more.

She also recently started to paint under the alias ©Ruach. The Facebook page is RUACH, which means "Breath of God." Under this alias, she will endeavor creations in a multitude of genres.

Look for her newly updated website *www.rutcreations.co*, as well the first ©Rut book. This project is underway with an invitation to all to participate in the creative journey!

Please email her at *info@rutcreations.co* if you are interested.

About the Developmental Editor

Jen Violi

Jen Violi is the author of *Putting Makeup on Dead People*, a BCCB Blue Ribbon Book, and finalist for the Oregon Book Awards.

As a mentor, editor, and facilitator, Jen helps writers unleash the stories they're meant to tell, from blogs to websites to award-winning books. Jen specializes in helping women access a deep well of joy from which to write stories of healing and transformation.

With advanced degrees in creative writing and theology, and certification in the Gateless method, Jen has facilitated retreats and workshops for twenty years and mentored and nurtured hundreds of writers as they find their voices, hone their manuscripts, and take creative dives and leaps.

Jen's writing has been featured in *Sweatpants & Coffee, Lady/Liberty/ Lit, Nailed Magazine, Mookychick, The Baltimore Review, Annapurna Living* and more.

About the Author and Compiler

Brenda Hammon

International keynote inspirational and motivational speaker, entrepreneur, philanthropist, international best-selling author, international award-winning writer and equestrian Brenda Hammon kicks down the walls of silence surrounding abuse. Brenda is a catalyst for finding "your" happy and has been called an "adversity expert" and has shared her experience on many stages.

Brenda is a storyteller of true life events that everybody is afraid to talk about openly, but wants to read about.

Brenda is the CEO and founder of Sacred Hearts Rising (*www.sacredheartsrising.com*) and also Spirit Creek Publishing (*www.spiritcreekpublishing.com*).

In denial of the ways abuse had permeated her life for forty years, Brenda suffered in silence and isolation, until finally taking a stand and dealing with her past. Known for her integrity, courage, and directness, Brenda now works to show others who have been abused that they too have a voice and can take back control of their lives. Brenda takes pride in breaking the cycle of abuse in her own family and speaking out loud to prevent the suffering of other children.

Not one to shy away from a challenge, Brenda decided to break the cycle of silence around topics that are not talked about openly in our society.

Also an award-winning rider and trainer, Brenda has competed on the National Circuit in dressage in Canada. With competing behind her, Brenda simply focuses on enjoying and bonding with her horses Hughie and Miss Mini Cooper.

With over two decades of experience in the insurance industry, Brenda and her husband Bud continue to run their own successful insurance business. They also offer training to other independent advisors through Spirit Creek Financial, and their M.G.A. which is designed for independent insurance advisors who are seeking mentoring, guidance, and assistance, and being the best that they can be. Brenda also served on the National Advisory Board for one of the leading lifestyle protection companies in Canada's insurance industry since the Advisory Boards inception.

Brenda makes her home with her husband Bud on their small farm outside of Alberta Beach.